LOVE!

Famous Canadians & the pets they love

by

Nancy Silcox

Ontario Veterinary College
University of Guelph,
Guelph, Ontario

For information about permission to reproduce selections from this book, write to:

OVC Pet Trust, Ontario Veterinary College, University of Guelph,
50 Stone Road, Guelph ON N1G 2W1

Charitable Registration Number: 10816 1829 RR 001

ovcpet@uoguelph.ca
www.pettrust.ca

Printed in the United States of America. Published simultaneously in Canada.

The text of this book is set in Bell Gothic Std.

Library and Archives Canada Cataloguing in Publications

Silcox, Nancy, 1949-, author
Live-Love! Famous Canadians & the pets they love / by Nancy Silcox

ISBN 978-0-88955-620-1 (pbk.)
1. Celebrities' pets--Canada. 2. Human-animal relationships--Canada. I. Title

SF411.5.S54 2014 636.088'70971 C2014-907073-X

Includes photo credits on page 227

Book and cover design: Jane Dawkins.
Original paintings for cover art: Tania Boterman
Live/Love Concept and Logo Design: Vopni & Parsons Design
www.vopniparsonsdesign.com

1 2 3 4 5 6 7 8 9 0

I dedicate this labour of love to
my husband Louis, who holds down
the Silcox fort...while I write, and
write, and write....

I also thank the many Canadian
pet lovers and protectors in this
book for inviting me into your busy
worlds to meet the four-footed
loves of your lives.

Contents

Preface

Here's a pop culture quiz. I'd like you to name three famous people with famous pets. "No problem," you report. "Queen Elizabeth and her Corgis. President Obama and his Portuguese Water Dogs. How about Paris Hilton and her Chihuahuas or Oprah Winfrey and her Golden Retrievers?" Easy!

The public's fascination with Hollywood, the American First Family and the British Royals is even surpassed if the celebrity comes with a four-legged companion.

Now let's direct the quiz to Canada. The game becomes harder. Chances are that, apart from Don Cherry's Bull Terrier Blue, and former prime minister Mackenzie King's Pat, his companion in journeys to the spirit world, most Canadians will draw a blank.

Books celebrating American celebrity pets abound too. They include The Dog Guide to Famous Owners; Very Important Pets; Celebrity Dogs; and Presidents and Their Dogs.

Not to be outdone by Hollywood and the White House, the British have countered with their own pictorial celebrations. Royal Animals: The British Monarchy and Pets by Royal Appointment; and The Royal Family and Their Animals are only a couple of U.K. books celebrating their love of pets.

And Canada? A thorough scouring of big box bookstores uncovers not a single tribute to famous Canadians and their pets. Why? National modesty? Our reputation towards understatement? It's high time to change the status quo.

xxx

A 2012 Ipsos-Forward survey on behalf of the Canadian Animal Health Institute indicates that 36 percent of Canadian households include at least one dog. The total number of canine pets is estimated at 6.6 million.

Statistics kept by the Canadian Kennel Club for 2012 list the Labrador Retriever as Canada's favourite dog. The German Shepherd, Golden Retriever, Poodle and Shetland Sheepdog fill out the top five of pedigreed canines. Canadian Living's 2012 survey of Canadian households with dogs lists the mixed-breed as our most common four-legged companion.

Well-known pet psychologist and behaviourist Dr. Stanley Coren at the University of British Columbia (and a contributor to this book) has compiled his "smartest dog" list. Coren names the Border Collie as top dog in the brains category. The busy Border is followed by the Poodle, German Shepherd, Golden Retriever and Doberman Pinscher.

And the least intelligent? Don't expect much from the regal but brainless Afghan Hound and the barkless Basenji. Beagles could use a dose or two of brain food too!

And what about the domestic cat? Not surprisingly, according to Ipsos-Forward, 37 percent of Canadian homes include at least one cat. With cat lovers more likely to have multiple pets, it's estimated that there are 7.9 million cats in Canada (excluding feral colonies). The common Domestic Shorthair is followed in popularity by the blue-eyed Siamese.

And while many might disagree, it appears that cats are as smart as dogs--but in a different way. Dr. Berit Brogaard, Ph.D. in his Psychology Today article of February 23, 2013 explains. Research on the cat's cerebral cortex, the part of the brain responsible for cognitive information processing shows twice as many neurons present as the dog's. So why can't they be trained to assist humans like dogs can? "Cats are more impulsive and have far less patience," says Brogaard.

xxx

In the summer of 2012, I approached the Ontario Veterinary College (OVC) at the University of Guelph with the idea of writing a long-overdue book featuring Canadian celebrities and their pets. OVC Pet Trust Fund would be the beneficiary of sales of the book.

OVC Pet Trust, founded in 1986 at the Ontario Veterinary College, University of Guelph is Canada's first charitable organization dedicated to the health and well-being of companion animals.

OVC Pet Trust honours the relationship between pets, their people and veterinary caregivers by raising funds to support innovative discoveries that improve the prevention, diagnosis and treatment of diseases of pets.

In the midst of a capital campaign to raise $15 million to open a state-of-the-art Companion Animal Cancer Centre, OVC and Dean Elizabeth Stone were delighted with my suggestion. They would gladly support and be the beneficiaries of my book.

Valued Pet Trust supporters, such as McDonald's Canada George and Susan Cohon; radio mogul Allan Slaight and his wife Emmanuelle Gattuso; broadcaster Brian Williams, television personality Valerie Pringle and Hockey Night in Canada's Don Cherry, came readily aboard the bandwagon.

Other celebrity pet lovers—entertainers, politicians, media types, business men and women, astronauts, writers and artists followed. Over thirty Canadian celebrities, from coast to coast, opened their homes and their hearts to me. All were bonded by an enduring love of their pets and a desire to lend their support to Pet Trust.

And what stories they had for me! From comedian Mary Walsh's hilarious tale of Bert the Freedom Dog, to artist Robert Bateman's memories of the rescue of a Mexican coatimundi; from "Man In Motion" Rick Hansen's hair-raising account of bicycle rides with his dog Magnus; to Jann Arden's cameo of the "purrcussion" cat Shrodie, these tales invite readers to laugh, to cry, to rejoice and to reflect.

Enjoy these adventures, as well as a collection of personal and family photos, that celebrate some of Canada's stars and their pets. You'll agree the owners' devotion to their "best friends" stands second to no one.

Alan, Angus, Jetta and Vegas

Victoria Nolan

Victoria Nolan's achievements in eduction and high-performance rowing would be considered exceptional for an able-bodied individual. Given that Victoria has a significant visual disability, her accomplishments become even more outstanding.

Diagnosed at 18 with retinitis pigmentosa (RP), a degenerative eye condition that results in loss of vision, Victoria continued on to university, completing a Masters of Childhood Education. She was consequently hired as a teacher by the Toronto District School Board.

After the birth of her two children, in 2003 and 2005, Victoria lost all but approximately 3 percent of her vision. The situation plunged her into despair. To counteract the effects of her loss, and to give her children a strong role model, Victoria took up competitive rowing.

She soon gained a position on the Canadian Paralympic Mixed Four rowing team. In 2007, her team took the Bronze medal in the World Rowing Championships. They won Gold in 2010 and Silver in 2011.

The team placed sixth at the 2008 Beijing Paralympics and seventh at the 2012 London Games.

xxx

Shortly after Victoria began rowing, she made the decision to acquire a guide dog. "I felt I needed a dog to help me manoeuvre through unfamiliar environments when I was competing away from home," she explains.

After considerable investigation, she came across the Fidelco Guide Dog School in Connecticut. A handler and the prospective service dog would come to her Toronto home for the training period. Fidelco worked only with the highly intelligent, trainable and fiercely loyal German Shepherds.

But her dog's "job description" would be vastly different than most in service roles. Travel would become an integral part of the dog's life. And so Jetta, a 20-month-old Shepherd, arrived at the Nolans' Toronto home in 2006 with his handler. But not all such service dog matches are made in heaven. "Jetta had anxiety issues, and it just didn't work out," Victoria recalls.

Jetta was followed by Angus, another Shepherd. He'd be trained to accompany Victoria to the Beijing Olympics where the Canadian Paralympic rowing teams were competing. It was a tough assignment.

> He'd need to stay calm and be reliable in chaotic airports. And because service dogs fly in the cabin of the plane at their human's feet, he'd have to sit still for hours on end. We were headed to China after all.

There would be toilet issues on long flights. Service dogs are trained to relieve themselves on special absorbent pads. But whether they follow their training is another thing.

> Angus refused to relieve himself on the pads, despite my and the flight attendants' encouragement. It had been so well engrained in him not to urinate indoors that he just wouldn't. But the minute his feet touched the ground when we landed, he had relief!

Angus had a few other issues too. "He was a barker and when a German Shepherd starts to bark they can appear intimidating and aggressive," states Victoria. When Victoria returned home after the Paralympics, she made the decision to try for a service dog with less "presence" than Angus.

xxx

Victoria's third Shepherd, Vegas, also came from Fidelco. It was a serendipitous match. Over the next four years, the two travelled throughout North American and Europe to compete. The bond between the two grew strong, as Vegas showed none of the anxiety and aggression issues of his predecessors.

As she travelled, Victoria discovered that she was in the minority of visually impaired athletes. Few brought their service dogs to competitions. She'd encountered only one dog attached to a member of the American rowing team. Some of the minor issues that developed with Vegas perhaps answered why they were in short supply. Adjustment to time zones was one.

> We were in Europe, and a teammate and I were sharing a room. In the middle of the night, Vegas thought it was time to play. He dropped a tennis ball on her face while she was sleeping and wanted to play. Luckily she loved dogs and thought it was cute!

Vegas didn't like being separated from his human either. Initially, he'd remained tied in the boathouse when Victoria left for the warm-ups, then on to the race. But he was one unhappy pup!

> During a meet in Poland, he was so eager to get to me that he broke the tie-down cable and ran over to us while we were carrying the boat! After that I started leaving him in my hotel room with the TV on to ease his anxiety.

xxx

Once racing season was over, Vegas took on another role. Victoria, a Special Education teacher at Gledhill Public School in Toronto, counted on him to assist her manoeuvre around the two-story school. She's one of only a few legally blind teachers in the Toronto District School Board, and the only one with a guide dog in the classroom.

Confident that she serves as a role model for her students, most of whom struggle with various disabilities, Victoria states: "I think my impairment helps them. They see that if I can overcome my problems, so can they."

Vegas became a well-loved fixture in her classroom. He proved to be therapy for her kids who struggled in school. "When he's out of his harness, the kids are allowed to pet him and brush him in class, and they love that."

And like most "regular" service dogs, Vegas has been Victoria's eyes in public, on the streets, and in stores as she shops.

> He dodges in and out of people and objects that are in my path, gently pulling me with him as he walks. He alerts me to stairs or dangers by stopping. And he locates things for me when I ask him, such as doors, stairs or elevators.

Victoria calls him "competitive" with slow walkers ahead of them.

> Vegas likes to be in the lead position of the pack. When we're walking on the street, I can tell when someone is a little in front of us because he picks up the pace until he passes them. Then he returns to his regular speed!

As Vegas reached his "middle age" of seven, he started to develop health problems and needed regular medication. Victoria made the decision in the spring of 2013 to retire him.

> A family member who has a farm was happy to have him live with him. So now he's just a pet and doesn't have to deal with the kind of stresses that service dogs are often subjected to. He's happy and his health problems are much improved.

It was difficult for Victoria to complete the final months of school without her faithful Vegas. She looked back fondly on their partnership: "Vegas was my eyes and my independence for the last five years. I completely trusted him with my safety and he proved time and time again that he was watching out for me."

xxx

In the summer of 2013, she travelled to Oregon to welcome a new service dog. She'd previously decided to switch breeds from German Shepherds to a Labrador Retriever. The decision came after a shocking incident in Toronto when she was asked to leave a convenience store, despite telling the employees that Vegas was a service dog.

> I think that people are more intimidated by the German Shepherd breed than the more common breeds used for service dogs, like Labs or Golden Retrievers. They associate Shepherds with police work, and the dogs seem to intimidate many people.

Victoria describes her service dog, Alan, as "the sweetest, most gentle, smart dog I could ever hope for." He's adjusted well to Victoria's classroom and is learning routines quickly. "With the help of dog treats," Victoria adds.

Alan won't be doing as much travelling as his three predecessors though. Victoria has retired from competitive rowing and she's taken up tandem bicycling. The first major test of her abilities was a 140-kilometre fund-raising tandem bicycle trek from Toronto to Collingwood in support of the Charity Foundation Fighting Blindness. While competitive cycling remains at the fun stage presently, she won't rule out competition in the future.

For a gal who called herself "clumsy and non-competitive" as a child and teenager, Victoria Nolan's achievements have become gold.

Albert and Jack

Chris and Helene Hadfield

A Sarnia native raised in Milton, Ontario, Chris Hadfield made the decision at age nine to become an astronaut. It was a bold pronouncement because at that time astronauts needed to be American to fly with NASA.

At 16, he met Helene Walter of Oakville. Helene had youthful goals too—to become an actress. But she traded them in after high school to study accounting at Ryerson University.

By then, Chris was off to the Royal Military College where he earned a degree in Mechanical Engineering. In 1981, the couple married. Chris was 22; Helene 21.

While Helene worked in the computer industry, Chris earned his stripes in the Canadian Forces as a fighter pilot. Over the next ten years, the Hadfield family, which now included three children: Kyle, Evan and Kristin, would adjust to frequent moves. Helene calls these years "tough" since she often coped with raising a young family solo.

A carpe diem–type of woman, Helene used these relocations to expand her own horizons. She took courses at law school, worked for motivational speaker Tony Robbins and learned to ride a horse.

In June 1992, Chris was selected to become one of four new Canadian astronauts to fly with the Canadian Space Agency. The family now relocated to Houston, Texas, the home of NASA's Johnson Space Center.

In 2001, Chris' dream took on a Russian flavour when he became director of operations for NASA at the Yuri Gagarin Cosmonaut Training Centre in Star City, Russia. Now he and Helene divided their time between Houston and Star City.

NASA's second space shuttle mission to rendezvous and dock with the Russian Space Station Mir saw Chris becoming the first Canadian mission specialist, and the first Canadian to operate the Canadarm in orbit.

At the conclusion of Chris' Russian assignment, Helene began a mission of her own—to become a professional chef. She studied full-time for two years at the Art Institute of Houston in the Culinary Arts program. Helene graduated at the top of her class.

Commander Chris Hadfield's accomplishments reached their pinnacle in 2013 when he became the first Canadian to command the International Space Station (ISS).

Committed to sharing the space experience with "earthlings," Commander Hadfield regularly tweeted information and observations to an eager public. Video link-ups between schools across Canada and the ISS were a regular occurrence too. And in the process, Chris Hadfield became an undisputed media star.

On his return to earth in May 2013, he resigned from government service to take on new challenges. These have included writing a book, An Astronaut's Guide to Life on Earth, and becoming a CBC news correspondent. He will also take up a teaching position at the University of Waterloo.

And after 26 years as "vagabonds," Chris and Helene Hadfield have settled down. They purchased a 60-year-old home in Toronto. Helene added house decorating to her long list of accomplishments and is eager to renovate.

With their children living on their own, Chris and Helene are adoring "parents" to two dogs: Jack, a Maltese, and a Pug named Albert.

xxx

When Chris and Helene Hadfield made the decision in 2013 to put down roots after more than 25 years of nomadic living across Canada, the U.S. and Europe, they had two prerequisites for location. Helene explains:

> First, we wanted to live in Toronto, which we think is just the best city in the world to call home. Second, our house had to be close to a large park where the dogs could run and play.

"Yes," Helene laughs heartily. "We bought this home for our dogs!"

XXX

Married for more than 30 years, Chris and Helene have never been without pets. Various cats have graced the family home, but dogs have taken precedence. This is no small commitment, considering their peripatetic lifestyle while Chris was working to achieve his childhood dream of being a NASA astronaut. Helene adds:

> And we're proud to say that in all those years, our dogs have never been kennelled. We've always had people living with us, so when we needed to be away, the dogs had caregivers they knew well.

When the Hadfield children were small, Labrador Retrievers were a natural choice for a kid-friendly pet. Troy, the yellow Lab, was oldest son Kyle's special friend and the two would regularly head off to a nearby park to play. Helene recalls:

> They had a routine. Troy would watch Kyle as he climbed up the steps of the slide. As soon as Kyle got to the top, Troy would run around to the front to be there when Kyle slid down to the bottom.

This manoeuvre was repeated countless times. Then one day Kyle arrived back home without Troy.

> "Where's Troy?" I asked right away. "Did you leave him at the park?" So we went back together to find the dog. And there was Troy waiting at the bottom of the slide as other kids came

> down. I guess somehow Troy had missed Kyle's turn sliding down and he was faithfully waiting until his boy came down.

xxx

No matter where the family was living they looked forward to time at the family cottage on Stag Island, on the St. Clair River near Chris' hometown of Sarnia. From Houston, where the family lived between 1992 and 2013, it was a gruelling 23-hour drive.

One year, with Chris training for a space mission, Helene set off on her own—as she often did. Elderly Lab Logan, and Jack, a young Maltese, were with her. Stopping the night at a motel along the way, Helene and the dogs settled in for a night's sleep before they drove the final leg of the trip. Helene recalls:

> The dogs and I were up at five a.m. the next morning to get on the road. Before we got in the car, I took the dogs, off leash, out to a grassy area beside the motel. And not too far away, the dogs spotted a cat—or what appeared to be a cat. Logan, being a Lab, took off after it; Jack, a lapdog, stayed beside me.

"Logan was never a good decision maker," offers Chris, with a laugh.

Not until Helene heard yelping did she realize that the "cat" had sported a stripe on its bushy tail. "And poor old Logan got skunk-sprayed right in the face," says Helene. With no de-skunking supplies on hand at such an early hour, and no stores open at dawn, Helene decided her best course of action was to load the dogs into the car and drive.

"I just wanted to get to the cottage as soon as possible," she explains. But with an eight-hour drive still in front of her, there would be pain ahead. "It was miserably cold out, so keeping the window open wasn't an option."

Arriving at Duty Free at the U.S.–Canada border, Helene made a quick trip inside. When she arrived back, it was soon apparent that Logan had presented her with another "gift." The trauma of the skunk encounter and the car ride had played havoc on his bowels.

"And he'd had explosive diarrhea," reports Helene. "All over him, and all over the back of the van. The best I could do was roll up the car mats and chuck them into a garbage pail."

No doubt the aroma coming from the Hadfield vehicle was a factor in the driver's lickety-split wave through Canada Customs.

XXX

Chris and Helene's move into the small-dog set came about by default. Their daughter, Kristin, had wanted a powder-puff Maltese ever since her childhood. As a gift after her high school graduation in Houston, Chris bought his delighted daughter her long-wished for dog. She named him Jack.

Kristin's decision to attend Queen's University meant that Jack would need to remain with the family in Houston. A university residence was no place for a young pup. By this time Chris and Helene had taken a real shine to the spirited ball of fluff, as Helene admits.

> The more I thought about maybe Kristin moving to an apartment for the rest of her university life, and taking Jack with her, the sadder I became. I had absolutely fallen in love with him. So we had a heart-to-heart chat and I asked her how she felt about Jack becoming Mom and Dad's dog permanently.

And so, Jack the Maltese came to stay.

Albert, a Pug, joined the family by similar default. Kristin's boyfriend had gifted her with a Pug as a graduation present from Queen's. Then Kristin was accepted for graduate school in Ireland. What would be the fate of dear Albert?

"With the quarantine issues bringing dogs into the British Isles, we persuaded her to leave Albert with us—at least temporarily," explains Helene.

And following a well-worn path, Chris and Helene fell in love with the comical pooch, whom Helene compares to a "savant." "You know how savants have learning deficits, but they are gifted in another area? That's Albert."

Albert's gift? His charming personality, says his "mom." "He's not the world's most intelligent dog but he has the 'IT factor'! Within five minutes of anyone meeting Albert they want a Pug," she laughs.

In the process of taking ownership of Kristin's dogs, both Hadfields have become confirmed small-dog converts.

> If you've had a large dog and then get a small one, you never go back to the big guys. Everything is just so much easier with them, especially if you travel. Small dogs ride in the airplane cabin and are welcome in many hotels.

The Hadfield dogs often accompany them into some stores too. "They'll sit right up in the child seat of a cart when we're in stores like Home Depot," reports Helene. She's been known to take her business elsewhere if a store won't invite her dogs in.

So it came as no surprise that the major life decision about where to buy a house and "nest" after Chris' retirement from NASA was made with the dogs in mind.

"As soon as we saw the house with the park across the street we both said 'SOLD.'" From past experience, the couple appreciates that dogs also facilitate getting to know new neighbours.

"But you learn their peoples' names long after you have gotten to know them as 'Muffy's Mom,'" Helene says, with a broad smile.

LOVE!

Albert, Alice, Chester, Edward, and Victoria

Farley and Claire Mowat

In 1969, writer Farley Mowat and his wife, Claire, journeyed from their home in Port Hope, Ontario, to the Magdalen Islands in Quebec. Farley was on assignment to this archipelago of eight island jewels, perched at the mouth of the St. Lawrence River. He was working with the CBC to make a documentary on lobster fishing there. Claire, trained as a graphic designer, was then starting what would become a successful career as a memoirist.

The couple so fell in love with the windswept Magdalen landscape, the people and the culture that they bought a home there. When the warm winds of summer came calling, Claire and Farley closed up their Port Hope house for a few months of spiritual renewal at their island retreat.

Over the eight years, from 1969 to 1977, that Farley summered on the Magdalens, he published a total of nine works, including Sibir: My Discovery of Siberia in 1970, A Whale for the Killing in 1972 and The Snow Walkers in 1975. Claire wrote her first book there, The Outport People. It chronicled the five years in the 1960s that she had spent in the outport community of Burgeo, Newfoundland.

xxx

The Mowat dogs, two large Labrador–Newfoundland crosses named Victoria and Albert always knew when their humans were packing for the long trip to the Magdalens. They were as excited to get to their summer home as were "mom and dad."

The fresh, salt air did wonders for the constitution—human or canine, for in the Magdalen summer of 1971, Victoria became pregnant by Albert. Farley and Claire eagerly anticipated the birth of the puppies.

The Mowats welcomed a steady stream of friends, relatives and colleagues, both famous and "everyday," to their summer home. That same summer, Prime Minister Pierre Trudeau and his wife, Margaret, arrived by helicopter for a visit with the Mowats. Margaret was pregnant too. She was carrying the couple's first child.

"As soon as Margaret met the dogs and heard about Victoria and Albert's puppies, she said she'd love to have one of the puppies when they were ready to be adopted," says Claire. The Trudeaus left for Ottawa excited about the two new members of the family that would be arriving.

A week after the Trudeau visit, Victoria gave birth to a litter of eight jet-back bundles of fur and feet. They would be ready to go to their new homes in October. The Mowats found homes for six of the pups, including the prime minister's new member of the family. This furry bundle was delivered by a Mowat friend to 24 Sussex Drive. Another pup found its way to Moscow, Russia. Russian prime minister Alexy Kosygin had been another Mowat visitor and had fallen under the puppy-spell too.

On Christmas Day of 1971, Margaret Trudeau gave birth to the couple's first child, Justin. His first pet had famous "parents" too.

xxx

"And we decided to keep two pups—a male and female," says Claire. In keeping with the royal theme, these were named Edward and Alice. Shepherded and tutored by the vigilant Victoria and Alice, the pups thrived and grew faster than spring violets.

One day, Farley made a shocking discovery. "I realized that both dogs were deaf," recalls Farley. A visit to a local veterinarian confirmed his suspicions. In her memoir, Travels with Farley, Claire recounts their realization:

> We anguished what to do. Both were smart, affectionate

> and obedient young dogs and most of the time one would ever have known they were deaf. By observing what...we humans did, they managed to fit into our lives almost as well as dogs that could hear.

"Nevertheless," Claire continues, "the prospect of coping with two deaf dogs, as well as Victoria and Albert, with our own peripatetic life, was daunting." They were particularly concerned for the pups' safety once they returned to Port Hope, just east of busy Toronto. How would the pups cope with the hurly-burly of street traffic when they couldn't hear danger coming?

The Mowats decided to keep Edward, but once they returned to Ontario, they would find a safer home for Alice. And what better environment for her than at the Ontario School of the Deaf in nearby Belleville?

One of Farley's first tasks after arriving in Port Hope was to write a letter to Dr. Demeza, the superintendent of the Ontario School for the Deaf (renamed The Sir James Whitney School for the Deaf in 1974). "I asked them if the school would consider taking Alice for their mascot," says Farley.

The school immediately agreed and Alice was delivered by Farley himself. Claire recalled her feelings as her "baby" left the house for the drive to Belleville:

> When it actually came time to part with little Alice, I couldn't stop weeping. I am sure I felt as sorrowful as any parent of a deaf child who was headed off to a special school to learn how to live with a disability. In a way it was worse, because Alice would not be returning to us at the end of term.

It was consolation to both Claire and Farley to get updates on how well Alice was fitting into the school environment. The good-natured pup was immediately beloved by students and staff alike, and quickly learned commands by ASL (American Sign Language), the conventional way of communication for students.

And no ordinary Alice was she, but the distinguished Alice Mowat Whitney. At night she patrolled the halls of the girls' residence; by day she had the run of the grounds. On weekends and holidays, Alice went home with her primary caregiver.

A chain-link fence enclosed the school property, so there was no danger of deaf Alice getting out into traffic. Those vehicles within the grounds were aware of Alice's presence and always drove with an eye out for a large black dog.

But one morning in May of 1979, when Alice was let out of the dormitory, she encountered something novel. The gate leading to the school grounds had been left open. Alice was curious and she wandered outside the property.

Unable to hear the sounds of traffic or know of its danger, she darted into traffic. Alice was struck by a passing car. By the time her presence was missed and a search party was mounted, the school's beloved mascot had died of her injuries. Students and staff were bereft at her loss.

XXX

Alice was buried in a grove of trees behind the school and a tombstone was erected to mark her grave. Later a portrait of her was commissioned. Through both markers, subsequent students learned the story of the school's mascot, and Alice's legend continued to live on.

Over the years, Alice's grave marker broke into several pieces. Students who had only known of the gentle black dog through legend were troubled and collected the pieces to be housed in the school archives. In 2009, a new marker was created and placed over Alice Mowat Whitney's grave.

Alice's memory is perpetuated to the present day. Each year the Whitney School holds an "Alice Day." In May of 2013, a new portrait of their dearly loved, long-departed mascot with one of her handlers, Rosemary Ryer, was unveiled. It hangs prominently in the school.

xxx

Over their fifty years of marriage, Farley Mowat, now 92*, and Claire, 81, have shared their love and their lives with seven dogs. Their most recent companion, the beloved Chester, died in his sleep in October 2012. He was in his 14th year. "We still miss him very much," both Claire and Farley admit. They treasure the photo taken of Farley and Chester at their Cape Breton Island summer home in July 2002.

The Mowats yearn for another dog but consider their own age with the longevity of a dog's life. "If we could find someone who would take the dog as their own, so if something happened to us..." Farley Mowat's softly voice trails off.

*Farley Mowat passed away on May 6, 2014.

Atticus, Barney, George, Humphrey, Mo and Tucker

Valerie Pringle

Broadcaster Valerie Pringle is one of Canada's most recognizable faces and voices. Indeed, she has been selected as one of the "Fifty Famous Faces of Fifty Years of Canadian Television" by the Banff Television Foundation.

Valerie started her career with Toronto radio station CFRB after graduation from Ryerson University's (then Polytechnic) Radio and Television Arts program. She later moved to television, hosting the CBC current affairs program Midday.

Jumping to CTV in 1993, she became the co-host of Canada AM until 2001. Since leaving early morning television, Valerie has produced and hosted a wide range of programs, including Valerie Pringle Has Left the Building, a 31-episode travel series, and Kilimanjaro: The Meaning of the Mountain.

Valerie now spends much of her time in volunteer work. Among her various interests, she sits on the Board of the Centre for Addiction and Mental Health; the Ontario Brain Institute; and the Canadian Broadcast Museum Foundation. She is a spokesperson for the Canadian Foundation for AIDS Research and is co-chair of the Trans Canada Trail Foundation.

She lives in Toronto with her husband, Andy, and her two chocolate Labrador Retrievers, Mo and George.

XXX

Valerie Pringle's laugh is infectious. And when she's talking about her beloved dogs, she laughs often, and hearty. As dogs have been a fixture in her life since childhood, she's had considerable occasion to have her funny-bone tickled.

The first dog-funnyman to catch hold of her heart when she was growing up was Barney the Beagle. Barney was a neighbourhood legend around his home base in the Yonge and St. Clair area of Toronto. "Dogs weren't leashed in those days," says Valerie, "and Barney took full advantage of this freedom." Daily he'd leave the Pringle home to visit with his neighbourhood favourites.

> He had a route he'd follow. He'd drop in at this store for a visit—and no doubt some treats and ear scratching. Then he'd go across the street to that one. We had no idea who was part of Barney's secret life.

In any case, what Valerie names "the legend of Barney" was so powerful that when neighbourhood kids arrived at her family home on Hallowe'en, it was more the chance to see where Barney lived than what was put in their treat bag!

And it wasn't just kids who looked out for Barney. Valerie tells the tale of her father returning home from work one day, and rear-ending a car in front of him. That driver had suddenly slammed to a stop to miss a dog he knew, crossing the street.

> The cause of the accident was none other than Barney, making his daily rounds. Dad saw the wisdom of not letting the guy he had hit know that it was his own dog that was the cause of the kerfuffle.

So endearing was Barney the Beagle that total strangers looked out for him. Valerie recalls with delight the day that he arrived home in a cab.

It was time for Barney to come in so Dad went outside to call. Just then a taxi drove up to our door. The car door opened and out hopped Barney! Apparently he'd been foraging around the Ports of Call Restaurant and the cab driv er spotted him.

The cabbie went inside and asked around if anybody knew about the beagle hanging around outside. Of course people did, as the restaurant was near our neighbourhood. So the cab driver put Barney in the back seat of his car an drove him home.

Valerie counts this Barney tale as yet another example of the rascal's charmed life. The measure of Barney the Beagle's greatness came, ironically, the day after he died, at a ripe old age.

It was Christmas and a neighbour knocked at our door with a present for Barney. It was a steak. My parents didn't know whether to just thank him for his present, keep it and eat it ourselves, or give it back to him with the sad news that Barney had died.

XXX

In the early years of her marriage to Andy Pringle and the birth of their three children, Valerie went dog-less. "And it just didn't feel right," she admits. As soon as the baby dust settled, she was back in business. Andy's mother was a big fan of Labrador Retrievers and Valerie soon joined the Lab fan club.

"I particularly liked the big, square and stocky English-bred Labs—dogs where you could get a real eyeful and handful," she says. And she'd fallen in love with the Chocolate variety.

But appearance was only part of Lab-appeal. Valerie was hooked by their sweet personality and earnest desire to please. She laughs: "And when you add food into the mix, they'll dance on their toenails for you."

She did her homework, visiting various breeders before settling on a pup. And so the spectacular Humphrey, a Chocolate Labrador Retriever, came to live with the family of five. After Humphrey came the magnificent Atticus, named after the noble Atticus Finch in "To Kill a Mockingbird."

> Atticus was absolutely the most handsome Lab, with the best temperament I have ever seen, to this day. We'd never bred one of our dogs before, but we decided that it was a shame to keep Atticus' great genes all to himself. So we bred him.

The female Lab lived with a breeder in Walkerton, Ontario. And in due time, a healthy litter of little Chocolate Atticuses was born. A drive to see the babies convinced the Pringles that one of Daddy's "babies" needed to come home with them. And so Tucker joined the household with his dad.

"We had great fun telling Atticus: 'Here's your son, old man, now you teach him well.'" Valerie takes delight in recalling Atticus' initial gruffness with his offspring; then, day by day, he allowed his son to creep a wee bit more into his personal space...until the two were inseparable.

But a two-dog household did have its moments of chaos.

> The doorbell would ring and it would set the dogs off—barking, jumping up at the door and generally acting like fools. I'm sure whoever was at the door thought they were entering a hunting lodge.

Given the food-obsessed proclivities of the breed, it follows that some of Valerie's anecdotes revolve around CHOW. Tinged with humour now, they were angst-causing at the time.

> It was November and Atticus was bringing up green bile. Clearly, he was sick, so he was off to the vet. They did

> x-rays and ultrasound, but the tests came back inconclusive. The vet suggested opening him up. So we went ahead with it.

Valerie reveals what was found. "It was a corn cob that the old garburator had scarfed down months earlier at the cottage. It had lodged in his digestive tract undigested, and was just festering away." Once the offending food source was removed, Atticus was bright-eyed and bushy-tailed.

Like father, like son, seemed to be the status quo. Tucker once consumed a Brillo pad, which necessitated veterinary care. "It was probably covered with the leavings of a fondue pan or something else yummy," suggests Valerie.

Valerie is a firm believer that despite the headaches of dog-parenting, pets are invaluable partners in the child-raising process. "Dogs teach children so many life lessons—like taking responsibility, and kindness, and above all the joys of unconditional love." Past memories of the love between her dogs and her growing kids bring a tear to her eye.

> The kids absolutely adored Atticus. He was the best gift we, as parents, ever could have given them. I can still remember one of my sons hugging his dog, and saying: "Mom, Atticus is my best friend."

xxx

The current Pringle Chocolate Labs are Mowbray, "Mo," age nine, and George, a baby at two. True to the breed, these dogs bring Valerie great joy. "They each have their funny quirks," she says—and breaks into a wide smile.

> When Mo is listening to you, he'll turn one ear towards you and cock his head, like he's intent on what you have to say. And George...he's doing it now...lying on his back

> with his four feet in the air and his mouth wide open, white teeth gleaming, saying: "Please rub my belly, ple-e-a-a-se."

With the Pringle kids grown and Valerie now semi-retired, she's convinced she's become "a crazy dog-woman—empty-nester, home alone clutching my dogs to my heart." The dogs insist that she stay active: walks at least twice a day, and in the winter, cross-country skiing. The Pringles live part-time in Niagara-on-the-Lake. There, Valerie has joined the dog-park set. "It's a great way to meet people, to break into a new community," she says.

Asked if she ever considers another breed of dog, Valerie Pringle firmly answers, "NO. For me, Labs are the only dog." Still, she hedges when considering "colour-scheme."

> A friend of mine has the most gorgeous Black Lab I have ever seen. She calls him the George Clooney of Labs. So if she ever breeds him I might just consider branching out...

LOVE!

Bert the Freedom Dog, Gobber and Train

Mary Walsh

Comedienne, actor, writer and political satirist Mary Walsh was born in St. John's, Newfoundland. She began her show business career in radio, before joining the Newfoundland Travelling Theatre Company (NTTC). Out of this group, came the theatre company Codco. In the late 1970's Codco toured widely across Canada, into the U.S. and to England.

CBC took notice and Codco came to Canadian television. Mary acted in and wrote many of the Codco skits. When the group separated, Mary developed the satirical "This Hour Has 22 Minutes" for CBC. She was joined by fellow Newfoundlanders Rick Mercer, Cathy Jones and Greg Thomey.

22 Minutes became a hit and it remains on air today. Mary is no longer a show regular, having left to explore other creative ventures, including the series "Hatching, Matching and Dispatching", and "Mary Walsh: Open Book".

Film work has also filled out her extensive resumé. She has acted in "New Waterford Girl", "Mambo Italiano" and "Geraldine's Fortune". Mary directed and produced the film Young Triffie's Been Made Off With in 2006.

In 2013, she began touring Canada with her one-woman show "Dancing with Rage." It incorporates her many stage and television personas, including the outrageous Marg Delahunty, Princess Warrior. Marg's "ambush" of Toronto Mayor Rob Ford became a YouTube hit.

Mary Walsh lives in St. John's, Newfoundland, with her husband, Memorial University English professor Don Nichol, and her dog Gobber.

XXX

Not surprisingly, Mary Walsh's dog stories are tinged with dark humour. They begin with "Bert the Freedom Dog," a Christmas gift from her Codco colleague, Andy Jones. Bert earned his moniker from the fact that he was rarely leashed or contained. The situation led to various "dogly" escapades.

"If we were walking with him in downtown St. John's and passed an open door, Bert would wander in—especially if he'd seen a cat inside," recalls Mary. A trek outside the city brought excitement of another sort. Mary tells the story in her own inimitable style:

> Bert went off on his own as we walked around, but later we caught sight of him off in the distance swimming in the bay. "Oh look," I said to Andy, "Bert's found a couple of friends." There were two, what looked like sheepdogs, with him in the water.

Andy and Mary continued their leisurely stroll, delighted that Bert was having a sociable time. "We were young—and total idiots," Mary confesses.

Coming out of a store, they came face to face with a woman, a rifle cocked over her arm. From the look on the woman's face, she was "out for bear." "I'm lookin' for a dog," the woman snarled. "He's been bitin' my sheep and has driv' two of them into the water." Andy and Mary gulped.

> So that's who Bert's friends were. They weren't a couple of local dogs going for a swim with him in the bay. They were a couple of the woman's sheep he'd rounded up. We were idiots, totally idiots!

Despite Mary's love of dogs, she has a confession: "There's a part of me that's afraid of dogs too. I always wonder what's going on in their minds. What are they going to do next?" No doubt her reservations stem from a certain free spirit named Bert!

xxx

Later, living a vagabond show business life, Mary didn't have a dog. Then during her son Jesse's childhood, the lovely Train, a magnificent Blue Merle Collie, entered her world. Train's primary personality trait was her stunning good looks, says Mary. "Train didn't do much other than sit around, working at being beautiful."

Later when a St. John's friend was looking for homes for a litter of puppies—"part Maltese, part Bichon and part 'crackie' (a Newfoundland term for 'mixed breed, with a bit of sauciness')," she explains—Gobber entered Mary and Jesse's lives. The addition of a wild-and-woolly pup was clearly an inconvenience to the lovely Train, but certainly one she would not stoop to acknowledge.

> Train would let Gobber take food out of her own bowl, and not flinch a whisker. Train knew she didn't have to establish power over Gobber or anybody. She knew her beauty was her power and no other dog could match her. So why bother yourself mussing up your coat fighting over precedence?

Gobber had some interesting personality quirks too—ones that Mary took some time to adjust to. "I didn't understand Gobber at first. He only wanted to lie on my stomach and for hour after hour, have me scratch his belly." Mary likens Gobber's needs to "the dog's version of a heroin addiction."

> He'd follow me around the house, from room to room, hoping I'd sit down on the couch and scratch his belly. It kind of irritated me at first. "Why don't you just find a place to LIE DOWN, Gobber" I'd snap at him.

xxx

Mary's peripatetic schedule during this era of her life saw her commuting regularly between home in St. John's and Halifax where "This Hour has 22 Minutes" was filmed. She recalls the travelling road show that went with her. "Jesse, me, Train, Gobber, the turtle and the Siamese Fighting Fish. What an absolute ZOO!" she laughs heartily.

She recalls Gobber's "immense and overwhelming energy" while contained in transit, in his portable kennel. "He'd put out so much energy barking and jumping around that the carrying cage would lift right off the floor."

Today Mary Walsh's life is a more settled one. Train has passed, "buried under the big tree where she liked to lie, looking serenely beautiful." Jesse is grown and on his own. Mary shares her home in downtown St. John's with husband Don Nichol and Gobber, now a feisty senior citizen of 14.

Long gone is her feeling of uncertainty towards her beloved pet—who still loves nothing better than a protracted belly scratch. "And he still follows me from room to room waiting for one," Mary laughs.

> The term "familiarity breeds contempt" just doesn't apply to me. New things, people, situations, still make me uneasy. It's not until I've gotten used to them that fear turns to love, respect and acceptance.

And love is surely what Mary Walsh feels for her beloved Gobber. She cherishes the opportunity that she has had to care for a pet. "You just can't help but be moved by the great love dogs have for you," she says. "And we have the opportunity to give that love back."

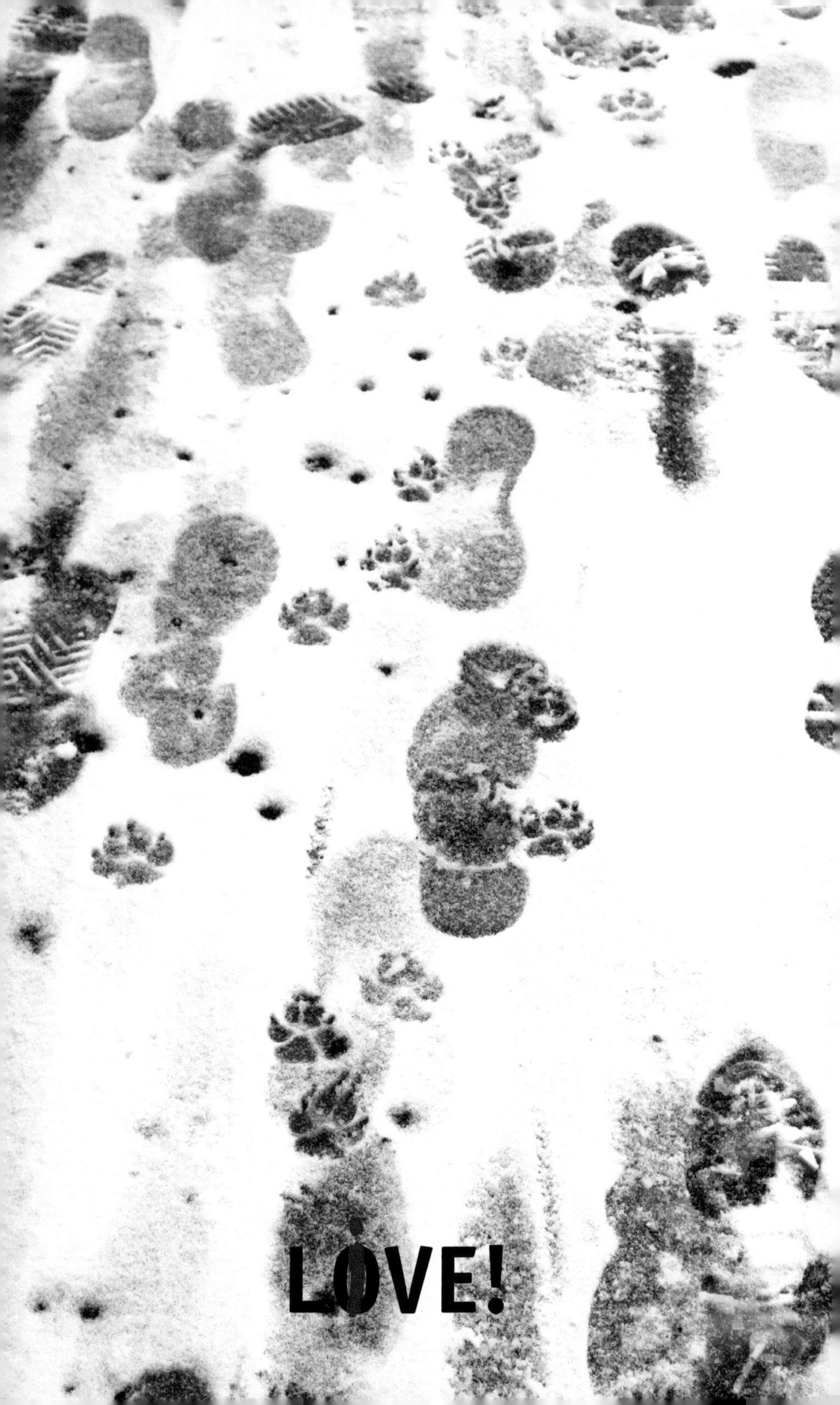
LOVE!

Bitz

Susan Musgrave

To call Susan Musgrave merely one of Canada's most celebrated poets is to shortchange her varied and multi-faceted accomplishments. She is a major force, cutting across Canadian literature and the arts: writing poetry, children's literature, fiction, non-fiction, even song lyrics. Lecturing in Creative Writing at the University of British Columbia rounds out a fulfilling professional life.

Susan's personal life matches her professional eclecticism. Growing up near Victoria, British Columbia, she was a high school dropout at age 14. Susan published her first book of poetry, Songs of the Sea Witch, at age 19. A period of vagabonding saw her living in California, Ireland and the Central American countries of Colombia and Panama.

During a stint as the Writer-in-Residence at the University of Waterloo, between 1983 and 1985, she received a manuscript from Stephen Reid, serving a 20-year sentence for bank robbery at Ontario's Millhaven Penitentiary in Ontario.

Their meeting culminated in their marriage in 1986, while Stephen was still in prison. His novel Jackrabbit Parole was released shortly thereafter. Susan and Stephen's life together was the subject of a 1999 CBC Life and Times documentary, "The Poet and the Bandit."

Drug addiction led him back to a life of crime and Stephen Reid returned to prison for armed bank robbery the same year. He was paroled in 2008, but freedom was revoked in November 2010 for drug use.

He remains at William Head Penitentiary on Vancouver Island where Susan visits whenever she can. She now lives on Haida Gwaii where she owns and manages Copper Beech Guest House near Masset.

Susan has had as many as seven cats living with her at any given time. Most of these arrive hungry, looking for a home. She currently shares her house with Boo, but other memorable cats in her life have been: Tiny Taan, Osama bin Kitten, Lishka, Sailah, Lucy, Ebba, Kitty Kitty, Basil, Mugsy, Ninja, Doogie and of course, Bitz.

Her story centres on Bitz, a very special friend.

xxx

"SOFTLY I GO NOW. PAD PAD" –Stevie Smith

Last fall I rescued (or so I believed at the time) a crazy tree-climbing cat from a life spent high in the windy branches of a hemlock on Haida Gwaii. I flew her south with me, to Vancouver Island; on Good Friday, in 2004, Bitz ran out onto West Saanich Road, smack into something you won't find in any treetop: a Honda Accord. The woman she'd hit, stopped. I found her standing in my driveway, crying, "I'm a cat person, too."

Bitz made it as far as the gate, fell at my feet, and lay, staring up at me. I wrung my hands; I prayed maybe she has just been stunned, though the trickle of blood at the corner of her mouth was a small grief with a short life, and a death, of its own. She died, twenty minutes later, in my daughter's arms, at the vet's.

Everything reminded me of her, from the can opener to the unused litter box, and went through me like a spear. In the garden I started digging a grave beside the last cat I loved who failed to look both ways—but then the lines of a poem, one by Robinson Jeffers, came flaring back: "To rot in the earth/is a loathsome end, but to roar up in flames—besides I am used to it/I have flamed with love and fury so often in my life...."

Bitz, who had spent her small lifetime reaching for the sky, would not have chosen the earth for a final resting place. I decided I'd have her cremated and take her home to Haida Gwaii where she could live again, in the wind, in the tree I spent most of last summer trying to entice her out of.

Over the next weeks I had to unload my grief on everyone I met. I remembered another poem by Lorna Crozier. In the poem, she has been crying for days over her cat and knows there are some humans she can share this with but others who will reply, "He's only a cat." The poet now divides people into these two camps. As Lorna explains, "It's one way of knowing the world."

She was "only a cat" and I had three others—older, wiser, more grounded (in all senses of the word)—to console me as I struggled to know the world again, any way I could. There were the people, too, who tried to comfort me with the familiar words we use when faced with someone else's loss. "All things must pass." "It was her time." "The only earthly certainty is oblivion." Few, I realized, could bring themselves to speak the word dead.

xxx

C.S. Lewis in "A Grief Observed" wrote about how his faith, even in God, was shaken when his wife died of cancer. "I look up at the night sky: is anything more certain that in all those vast times and spaces, if I were allowed to search I should nowhere find her face, her voice, her touch. She died. She is dead. Is the word so difficult to learn?"

She will live forever in your memory. Something else the well-meaning repeat. But live is precisely what Bitz would not do—ever again. All I had left of her was in ashes, and my unappeasable grief.

I tried revisiting her favourite places—as if it would bring her back to me—but it didn't help. Whether it was up on the shed roof (sometimes I would "rescue" her three times a day) or where she napped between my feet, on my office floor, she had become, everywhere, lost to me. "Death is a scatterer," wrote Stevie Smith. "He scatters the human frame/The nerviness and the great pain/Throws it on the fresh fresh air/And now it is nowhere."

When someone we love dies, we are told, "She is happy now, at peace, in God's hands." Wasn't Bitz in God's hands when she bolted onto the road? Or do His hands hold onto us more fiercely the moment we leave our body and fly off? And if so, why?

I have no good pictures of Bitz—she never stood still long enough when being photographed—and now two months later, already I can't remember her body in any detail. And yet it is her body, her particularity—the way she let me pluck her off the shed roof, the way she clung to me, all grateful, purring warmth, as we descended the ladder—I miss.

C.S. Lewis says passionate grief does not link us to the dead, but cuts us off from them. Grief makes the dead far more dead. Paradoxically, when we let go, the less we mourn, the closer to our lost one we will get.

And he gives good reasons for grief. "It comes from the frustration of so many impulses that have become habitual. Thought after thought, feeling after feeling, action after action have our loved one for their object. Now their target is gone. We keep on through habit fitting an arrow to the string; then remember, and have to lay the bow down."

xxx

Bitz, habitually, changed my life. She would be sleeping peacefully beside me on the couch; I'd be afraid to get up and return to my desk, knowing that, if I moved, she would follow. Thought after feeling after action—the daily rescue from the roof, the endless openings of cans of tuna, her waiting for me at the gate when I pulled into the driveway—had my scatterbrained cat for their object. Now she is gone. For me to move on will mean resetting my sights on a target much bigger than my boundless love.

She wasn't just a cat. She is dead. But I still picture the look she gave me as her eyes flamed up one last time in our driveway. Her look—of love, of fury—seemed to say, "We had great joy of my body. Now, scatter the ashes."

Blue

Don Cherry

As Terry Fox is to Canadian hero, the Group of Seven is to Canadian art and Sir Frederick Banting is to diabetes, Don Cherry is to hockey. And while wholly deserved, the label is ironic. Don Cherry played only one game in the NHL.

Born in Kingston, Don played junior hockey in the OHL before moving up to the American Hockey League's Hershey Bears. In 1955, he was called up to play with the parent Boston Bruins. He played one game, before being sent back to the minor leagues. He toiled there until 1970. Recurring injuries kept him from the big time.

Three months of odd jobs followed Don's retirement. He sold cars, worked in construction and painted houses to pay the bills. Then in late 1971, he was hired to coach the Rochester Americans of the AHL, a position he held for three years. He won Coach of the Year honours in the 1973-1974 season. For the last two seasons, he was also Rochester's general manager.

He was promoted to the NHL in 1975 and became head coach of the Boston Bruins. Over his five years in Boston, he was once named the NHL's Coach of the Year. After leaving the Bruins in 1980, Don coached the Colorado Rockies for one season.

Don began his broadcasting career as a CBC colour commentator for Hockey Night in Canada in 1980. The popular intermission spot Coach's Corner grew out of this.

A great lover and protector of animals, Don Cherry is indelibly associated with the dog he calls "the love of his life," a blue-eyed Bull Terrier named Blue. Now long departed, the original Blue has been followed by Blue II and Blue III.

xxx

Blue, a white English Bull Terrier puppy, scampered into Don Cherry's life in 1970, shortly after Don retired from playing professional hockey. He was then unemployed and his mood was low. Don hoped getting a dog would lift his spirits.

But not any dog. It had to be a Bull Terrier. Don had always admired the breed, with its muscular, solid-as-a-tank build, and its reserved but loyal-to-family temperament. He explains his preference:

> Bulls are known by a couple of names. One is the "Cavalier Gladiator" because of their bravery. The other is "The White Cavalier" because, despite their power and fearlessness, they will never attack a smaller dog.

He'd scraped together enough cash to purchase a pup and headed to a breeder in Long Island, New York. Little could Don Cherry have imagined how this visit would change his life. Among the litter was an anomaly—a female pup with blue eyes, considered a fault with Bull Terrier fanciers. But Don was mesmerized by the little one, and knew this was the dog for him. "The eyes made her personality mysterious. And I liked that." He decided to call her "Blue."

And so the charmer came home to live with Don and Rose Cherry. And mysteriously, Don's luck began to change. "I got a job in construction right after that, and a few months later I was hired to coach the Rochester Americans hockey team in the American Hockey League."

After three winning seasons with Rochester, Don made the big time. In 1974, he was named head coach of the Boston Bruins. "And I owed it all to Blue," Don insists. "Getting her changed my life."

xxx

With Don, the Bruins were getting two for the price of one. Blue became the mascot for the team. The dog's "tough-girl" appearance reinforced the team image of "the big, bad, brawling Bruins." The media loved Blue and lined up to get photos. One clever caption written over a photo of Blue read: "The Bruins are going to the Dogs."

Blue was photogenic, but true to the breed, she stayed somewhat aloof to those outside the family circle. There was only one exception to Blue's rule—Don's friend, NHL-er René Robert of the Buffalo Sabres. "Blue was crazy about René," laughs Don, "and would pay more attention to him than pretty well anybody else." But one day René made a fatal mistake.

> René snapped his fingers to get Blue's attention. Blue didn't like that one bit. It was like she wouldn't be taken for granted, that she was insulted to be called that way. And from then on, she ignored René like she did everybody else, except us.

Blue was a great car traveller and routinely tagged along with Don when business took him to different cities. He drew the line with flying though. "I'd never put her through that experience."

So when Don got a call one day from the Miller Brewing Company inviting him and Blue to appear in a television commercial, a gig that necessitated air travel, Don gave it little thought. "Blue was far more valuable to me than the money. So I turned down the twenty-five thousand dollars just like that."

XXX

A luck-changer Blue certainly was, but she was a role model and teacher too. Don recalls an incident at the family cottage to illustrate his point:

> Beside our cottage was a family who owned two huge Great Danes. Now Danes are supposed to be mellow but these two were vicious and had killed a Doberman Pinscher. One day they had me cornered too and I was lucky to escape without being mauled.

Don always kept the much smaller and lighter Blue far out of the Danes' territory. But one day, his safety system broke down and Blue was face-to-face with the "tough guys."

> There were the two Danes waiting for her between the two cottages. I saw it happen and thought my dog would be torn to pieces. But she didn't flinch; she held her own. The Danes backed off and went home. It was like they felt her courage and they respected her.

Don used Blue's story many times as an example of courage in the face of insurmountable odds.

xxx

At age 11, in 1981, Blue passed away. Don was devastated. "I lost my best friend," he says. Shortly after his dog's death, he was driving when Stevie Wonder's song "You Are the Sunshine of My Life" came on the radio.

> The words of that song just hit me and I broke down right there on the highway and wept. "You are the sunshine of my life; you are the apple of my eye." I had to pull over to the side of the road until I'd collected myself.

Other dogs, other Bull Terriers named Blue, have joined the Cherry household since the original. None have taken her place. "They're breeding Bulls to be all soft and sweet and friendly now," says Don, with some distaste. "Blue was reserved, and I liked that."

Don Cherry reflects on the gift of Blue over her 11 years of life:

> I could always depend on Blue to be there. Blue didn't care whether the team won or lost or what the press said. She was true. To go for a walk alone with Blue was good for the soul. And there'll never be another like her.

LOVE!

Charlie Pickles and Pork Chop

Lynn Crawford

Born and raised in Toronto, Lynn Crawford showed her artistic talents from an early age. After high school, she enrolled in George Brown's Culinary Arts program. Here Lynn felt truly at home, and she shone.

A stint travelling and more chef-learning in California followed college. Then she took up a position with the Four Seasons hotel chain in Montreal. From Montreal, it was up the Four Seasons chain of command to chef positions in Nevis, West Indies, and Vancouver. Lynn's star was on the ascendant.

A culinary coup was being named executive chef at the Four Seasons in Toronto, one of the city's premiere hotels. She made news again when later she was appointed executive chef at the Four Seasons in New York.

While living in the Big Apple, Lynn appeared on the Food Network's Iron Chef America series in a cook-off with chef Bobby Flay. But by 2009, she was looking for new adventures and returned to Toronto. She had ideas she wanted to explore.

Lynn appeared on several episodes of the Food Network's Restaurant Makeover, and in 2010, her Food Network series "Pitchin' In" debuted. The camera follows Chef Lynn as she travels to various food-producing venues across the U.S. and Canada, "pitchin' in" with the work. She invariably prepares culinary delights at the conclusion of the show using the targeted food for the episode.

The same year, with Chef Lora Kirk, Lynn Crawford opened the restaurant Ruby Watchco in the Riverside neighbourhood in Toronto. At Ruby Watchco, Chef Lynn practises what she preaches, serving food that is locally grown and harvested and creatively cooked to perfection.

Lynn Crawford lives in Toronto with her beloved dogs Charlie Pickles and Pork Chop.

XXX

Chef Lynn Crawford insists it only makes sense that somehow she'd bring food into her choices of pets. As such, this confirmed dog lover shares her Toronto home with a Chocolate Labrador Retriever and a Milk Chocolate Dachshund.

She'd make the connection even more vivid with the dogs' names. "This is Charlie Pickles, the sweetest dog in the world," she introduces. "Is she not the most beautiful, the most magnificent darling?" Yes, Charlie Pickles Crawford is female. "I just like Charlie for a name. Not Charles, not Char, Charlie. It just suits," she explains.

Keeping pace with the 80-pound Charlie Pickles is the diminutive Pork Chop. Still a youngster by dog standards, he's a smooth-coated Dachshund, in shades of creamy milk chocolate and burnished rust. Pork Chop's gleaming brown eyes promise that he's full of beans and puppy rascalhood. "He's a big personality trapped in a small body," Lynn says, with a laugh.

Despite the imposing size difference, it's clear that the two Crawford canines are the best of friends. "Pork Chop is the dominant one," Lynn explains. "Charlie Pickles is so laid back and kind, she lets the little stinker into her bowl."

It's clear too how much Lynn's pets mean to her. "They are my best friends, and I adore them," she states. Adoring them means taking good care of their needs: good food—but no Crawford gourmet dishes—lots of human companionship and exercise.

Chef Lynn is a busy woman, juggling a restaurant, a television show and personal appearances. So when she has to be away from the house, she relies on her righthand dog walker Katy.

xxx

Charlie Pickles and Pork Chop played a role in the production of Lynn's new cookbook At Home with Lynn Crawford: 200 of my Favourite Recipes. It hit bookstore shelves in September 2013. "The dogs will be very famous because of the book," Lynn predicts.

Staging and photography for the cookbook took place in the Crawford home kitchen. Present for the shoot were Lynn, her chef Lora Kirk, food and prop stylist Sasha Seymour, photographer Kathleen Finley and, of course, Charlie Pickles and Pork Chop.

"They were there as official taste testers, and unofficial food stylists," Lynn laughs. Many of the photos for the book were shot on the Crawford backyard deck—in Charlie Pickles' and Pork Chop's range. "There were more than a few photos we had to throw out, because there was a dog ear in one, or a dog nose in another," she says, with her patented "Crawford laugh." She points out a framed photo on her wall. It's Pork Chop inspecting the quality of a rack of pork loin, which is deliciously topped with apricots and cipollini onions.

Lynn has included a recipe for dog cookies in the cookbook. It's called "Ninja Dog Treats." A photo of whimsical Ninja-shaped goodies being inspected by Charlie accompanies it.

xxx

Hallowe'en is a big deal in Lynn's neighbourhood, with the famous chef herself leading the way in treat creativity. She sets up her "Green Egg" barbeque on the front steps of her home. Then she dresses the two dogs as hot dogs, dons a hot dog costume herself, and treats the kids to hot dogs and hamburgers. "I get a load of adults in the neighbourhood dropping by too," she says, with a smile.

Fun of another sort takes place at the newly purchased cottage in the Kawarthas. She'd wanted to take her pets with her on vacation and had found the pet-friendly Lake Edge Cottages, north on Lake Katchewanooka in the Kawarthas.

"It was lovely, close to the lake with a cozy fireplace, and a kitchen to prepare your food. And Charlie Pickles just loved jumping off the dock into the lake." The cottage experience was so good that she decided her dogs deserved even more.

"So I bought my own cottage—for the dogs. Now they can swim and have fun all summer," she explains, with delight. While he can't hold a candle to Charlie Pickles in the swimming category, Pork Chop will cool off in lovely Buckhorn Lake too.

Sense of family, good friends and fellowship burns bright in Lynn's soul. But the picture is incomplete without her furry family. "They bring so much pleasure into my life," she says. "I can't imagine a day without them."

LOVE!

Cindy-Bonkers, Cooper, Minnow and Spike

Arlene Perly Rae and Bob Rae

Born and raised in Toronto and educated at the University of Toronto, Arlene Perly was an established journalist before she added "politician's spouse" to her life experiences. For a number of years, she was the Toronto Star's reviewer of children's literature. She also wrote occasionally for the Globe and Mail, Quill & Quire and other publications.

Bob Rae began his political career as the NDP Member of Parliament for the federal riding of Broadview Greenwood. He later moved into provincial politics in the riding of York South and in 1982 was elected Leader of Ontario's NDP Party. The NDP was voted into power in the election of 1990.

In addition to her duties as premier's wife, Arlene reviewed children's literature. In 1997, Everybody's Favourites, her "Consumer's Guide to Children's Literature" was published.

A committed social activist too, with a particular interest in children's issues especially child poverty and child literacy, Arlene Perly Rae has sat on various boards of directors. They include World Literacy of Canada and the United Way of Greater Toronto.

The couple resumed their bi-city, Ottawa–Toronto, life when Bob was elected federally to represent the Liberal Party in Toronto Centre in 2008. He became interim Liberal leader in 2011. Bob Rae retired from politics in June 2013.

Parents to three daughters, Judith, Lisa and Eleanor, Bob and Arlene live in Toronto. They are devoted "dog grandparents" to Cooper.

XXX

Cats and dogs have long been a part of Bob Rae and Arlene Perly Rae's life. One of their first pets was a spirited Cockapoo affectionately known as "Cindy-Bonkers."

"Cindy was bonkers because she was very particular about whom she barked at, and when," says Arlene. "She barked at some men, but not all men, and some women, but only a few." Anyone with a uniform got Cindy-Bonkers' attention too, but they had to be standing. If the "uniform" sat down, the dog would stop barking."

Cats were an integral part of the family circle too. Minnow and Spike were both rescues. Minnow, proud and regal in bearing, had an active social life outside the family circle. When he wasn't holding court at home, he roamed the neighbourhood like a monarch making the rounds of his kingdom. Some of his "subjects" gave him treats, others a scratch around the ears or a rub. "The neighbourhood kids just loved Minnow," says Arlene.

Spike was the Daredevil, the Risk-Taker. Nothing was too high to climb, too broad to jump over; no new experience was too intimidating for this gal to explore. The "cats have nine lives" adage had been coined for Spike Rae. Despite her death-defying antics, Spike is still thriving at age 15.

But one family pet stands out above the others. The story mixes an affable dog named Cooper and the serendipity of social media.

XXX

The scene is set with Bob and Arlene away from their Toronto home attending Liberal Lawrence MacAulay's annual strawberry social in his home province of Prince Edward Island. It's a giant affair with hundreds of people in attendance. Bob, as leader of the Party, is kept hopping with official duties.

Sometime during the afternoon, Arlene's cell phone rang. It was the couple's youngest daughter, Eleanor. Arlene knew immediately from the tone of her daughter's voice that something was wrong. "Mom... Cooper's run off," reported Eleanor.

> It seems that Eleanor had been out for a walk with her gentle giant of a Bernese Mountain Dog and Great Pyrenees mix. There'd been a car accident on the street right beside them and Cooper, a usually placid and dependable fellow, was spooked by the kerfuffle. He'd pulled his head out of his collar and tore pell-mell down the street, across front lawns and around houses. Eleanor was in hot pursuit. Weighing just shy of one hundred pounds, this guy coul move and in the blink of an eye, Cooper had disappeared.

Eleanor kept searching around houses and garages, calling Cooper's name, but with no result. With panic rising, she called her two sisters and several friends to help in the search. She also placed a call to her parents in Prince Edward Island, hoping they might have some good ideas about how to broaden the Cooper hunt.

> After Eleanor's call, I told Bob what was going on. He was as worried as I was. Both of us felt terribly helpless and so far away. Over the next few hours all of us were in frequent contact with each other, passing search ideas back and forth.

Then suddenly Bob had an inspiration. "I'll put a message on Twitter," he suggested. Pulling out his trusty BlackBerry, he posted a "Lost Dog" message online. Serendipitously, he had a Cooper photo on his phone and this was posted along with the message. Ah, the wonders of modern technology!

Within an hour, Bob got a reply to his Tweet. It seems that Cooper was safe. He'd been found sitting on the porch of a house not too far from where he'd bolted. The family had taken him in.

Despite the absence of any identification or tags (they were attached to the abandoned collar), the rescuers knew that this big guy was surely someone's beloved pet. And, they reasoned, that "someone" was looking for him!

The finders decided to consult with their next-door neighbours about how to report a lost dog—one without any identification.

> But the neighbours had an even better idea than an ad. They searched online—Twitter, Facebook—for any "Lost Dog" postings. Lo! And Behold! There was one from Liberal Leader Bob Rae of all people!

Facebook facilitated the finders contacting Eleanor. She and her "posse" were still out beating the bushes for her lost dog, but they were regularly checking social media too. Eventually, the searchers and Cooper were reunited. Much hugging and face-licking followed.

It seems the loveable Cooper had made his mark with the family who found him even in the short time he'd been their guest, says Arlene. "The kids had already named him Charlie."

Companion animals play such integral roles in our lives. And when we lose one, even temporarily, our world falls apart. But thanks to technology, one lost dog, beloved by an entire family was found. All the Rae family, with a number of support cast, gave thanks to that serendipity.

LOVE!

Coquette and Monsieur Leo

Joannie Rochette

Joannie Rochette vaulted into the public consciousness through tragedy. Two days before she was to skate for a medal at the 2010 Vancouver Olympics, her mother, Therese Rochette, died of a heart attack. Putting her grief aside, Joannie chose to complete what she'd set out to do. Skating an outstanding and courageous program, she was awarded an Olympic bronze medal.

Born in 1986 in Montreal and raised in the town of île Dupas, Quebec, Joannie was on the skating rink by the age of 2, and taking lessons at 6. By age 14, she was moving up the Canadian skating hierarchy.

Joannie was only 19 when she won her first Canadian senior title. It afforded her a place in the 2006 Winter Olympics in Turin, Italy. Here Joannie placed a respectable fifth place. She continued to improve her performance at international meets. She earned a silver medal at the 2009 Worlds, becoming the first Canadian woman since Elizabeth Manley to do so.

Her Vancouver Olympic bronze medal was sweet sadness. That year Joannie Rochette was also voted Female Athlete of the Year by the Canadian Press.

A current member of the touring Canadian Stars on Ice troupe, Joannie loves skating for fun without the pressure of competition. She's a spokesperson for various charities, including the iheartmom campaign, a project of the University of Ottawa's Heart Health program. It works to raise awareness for heart disease in women.

xxx

Growing up an only child to Therese and Normand Rochette in a rural area outside Montreal, Joannie Rochette had lots of opportunity to play with barn cats. And she did—especially the kittens. But she desperately wanted a cat to keep her company inside the house too.

"But my parents thought animals belonged outside," says Joannie. One day a stray cat appeared on the Rochettes' porch. Further investigation found Mama had six tiny kittens hidden in a nest. Joannie pleaded with her parents to let the family come in—just until the kittens were older. She won her case, on the understanding that the felines would find new homes after they grew.

When moving time came, Joannie begged and pleaded—successfully—to keep the mother and one kitten. But as feral cats have a mind to do, one day Mama disappeared, never to be seen again. And so "Coquette" alone became young Joannie's special pet.

> She was lovely—black stripes with a brown nose and piercing yellow eyes. Most of the time she was gentle, but being a wild cat she could be fierce too. Every time the vacuum cleaner was turned on she'd hiss at it.

Like a typical cat she loved to sleep on her human's lap; but like a dog she'd run to greet her little girl when she came in the door from school. Or she'd follow Joannie around the property on a leash.

The bond between Joannie and Coquette loosened when skating took a larger place in Joannie's life. Now away for days, even weeks at a time, at skating competitions, Joannie found that when she returned home, Coquette had warmed to her father, Normand. "But she still always slept on my bed," recalls Joannie.

xxx

The Rochette household was in high spirits as the 2010 Vancouver Olympics approached. Joannie was favoured to win a medal and both Normand and Therese prepared to leave for Vancouver to see their daughter skate. It was there where Therese suffered her heart attack. She was only 55. Her mother's death devastated Joannie. But sure that Therese would want her to go ahead with her Olympic dream, Joannie plucked up her huge store of courage and did the skate of her life. She dedicated her success to her beloved mother.

The heartaches were not over for Joannie. Three weeks after her mother's death, Coquette passed away. The senior citizen was in her 19th year.

> Coming so close after Mom's death, I was heartbroken. She was so old and was really starting to have some health problems. I knew that she had had such a good long life, but I wish I had been able to be home to say goodbye to her.

xxx

Joannie remained pet-less for some time. Then unexpectedly she met with an experience that changed all that. "I was visiting with someone who had a Savannah cat and I fell in love with the breed," she recalls.

Joannie set to work learning about the beautiful Savannah—a hybrid cross between an African Serval and a domestic housecat. The Savannah's size depends on the degree of Serval genes. The largest, the F1 Savannahs, can reach 28 pounds and are from parents where one is a Serval and the other a housecat. Even the more petite F3, F4 and F5 Savannahs can tip the scales at up to 20 pounds—at least double the size of a housecat. When an F1 is bred with a housecat it produces an F2. When an F2 is bred with a housecat it produces an F3 and so on. With long legs, large ears and a spotted coat, the Savannah is spectacularly beautiful and exotic.

Personality-wise, they're highly active, intelligent and adventurous. More like a dog than a cat, they can be easily trained to a leash and love to fetch. Most Savannahs love water and some enjoy joining their owner in the shower!

Joannie and her boyfriend, Guillaume, travelled to Valleyfield, Quebec, to visit a breeder. They chose an F3 Savannah to share their home. They named him Monsieur Leo. Joannie describes him as "being like a dog—he follows us around the house." He's affectionate too, preferring to sleep at the head of his people rather than their feet. The Savannah's intelligence and trainability surpasses most ordinary housecats. The latter quality is proven by the progress M. Leo is making using the regular toilet rather than kitty litter. The couple believes this is cleaner for the house and for Leo's paws than using litter.

> We're training him to use the toilet by the Litter Kwitter system. An insert sits on the regular toilet and gradually, by careful training, he'll be able to use the toilet like humans do. And he's doing great.

With a laugh, Joannie notes that with curiosity being one of the Savannah's notable characteristics, M. Leo is fascinated by the movement of water. "So he sticks his head through the Litter Kwitter seat to watch the results of the flush," she laughs.

Whether M. Leo will have the same long lifespan as her dear departed Coquette, Joannie doesn't know. But of one thing she is certain. Being the guardian of a Savannah cat takes a lot more effort.

LOVE!

The Doras

Brian and Geraldine Williams

For almost forty years, one name has remained a constant in Canadian television sports and Olympic coverage. That name is Brian Williams.

Born in Winnipeg, and calling half-a-dozen U.S. and Canadian communities "home" in his youth, Brian attended Aquinas College in Michigan. There he majored in History and Political Science. But broadcasting had been a love since childhood and at Aquinas he hosted a campus radio show. After graduation in 1969, he combined time behind the microphone with his duties as a History teacher in a Grade 8 classroom.

Returning to Canada, Brian chose broadcasting as his long-term path. His career started at radio station CHUM in Toronto, followed by CFRB. In 1974, he landed a position as sports broadcaster for CBC. He served as play-by-play commentator and studio host for a wide variety of sports, from auto racing to professional football.

Brian Williams' long association with Olympic television coverage began at the Montreal Olympics in 1976. Between 1984 and 2006, he covered 12 winter and summer Olympics.

In 2006, Brian jumped to CTV and the sports network TSN. Here he has covered professional football and hockey, skating, golf, tennis and skiing. He headed CTV's Olympic coverage in Vancouver in 2010 and in London in 2012. In total, he has covered an impressive 14 Olympic games.

With his wife, Geraldine, Brian is devoted to his mixed-breed rescue dog, Dora.

xxx

I get a foreshadowing of Dora's personality the moment I ring the doorbell to Brian and Geraldine's North York home. A cacophony of spirited barking ensues before Brian opens the door and invites me inside.

"Dora! Shush," Brian orders, as his pint-sized companion continues her song. Geraldine joins us and urges Dora to be calm. The wee sprite is on her hind feet, adding dance to her melody. "Dora has anxiety issues," offers Geraldine, and bends down to scoop the bundle of black fur into in her arms. "She's always been like this."

Now at eye view, I can size up the little firecracker. Dora's a charmer, with black, shoe-button eyes, tidy snout and the most creative ears I've yet to see on any dog. One makes an attempt to stand at attention, while the other has given up entirely. It flops whichever way the wind carries it.

It's no wonder that this little rescue, from the province of Quebec, has captured the Williams' hearts.

xxx

Dora, also known as Dora II, is Brian and Geraldine's third dog. She follows in the paw-prints of a handsome Fox Terrier named Lucy, and Dora I, a mixed Poodle–Bichon. The Williamses have had their share of health concerns with both dogs. Lucy had bladder cancer and Dora I had an inoperable mast cell tumour.

And although it tired her, the plucky Dora I enjoyed her walks around the neighbourhood. "So when her energy started to flag, one of us would end up carrying her," says Brian. One serendipitous day, a solution presented itself to the outing dilemma.

> We were going past this house and here was a baby stroller, a Perego, in excellent shape, sitting at the curb. It looked

> like it was headed to the garbage. Geraldine suggested to me: "That would be perfect for Dora."

Polite, as well as resourceful, Brian Williams, one of the more recognizable faces in Canada, knocked on the door of the house that seemed to have produced the stroller. When the resident answered, Brian asked permission to take over ownership of the cast-off. "They were delighted to have us take it," recalls Brian. So now Dora rode in comfort and style when she was out for her constitutional.

XXX

After Dora I passed away, Brian and Geraldine gave thought to another dog. "But it had to be a rescue dog—small and non-shedding," says Geraldine. They spent hours, poring over images of dogs up for adoption at various shelters and humane societies across the country.

Then one day they found a treasure. The little mixed breed was presently at a shelter in Quebec. Geraldine recalls: "It was hard to see her little face in the picture. Her fur was black, but she had one ear that stood up and one ear that flopped. We fell in love with her."

The fact that the little darling was already named Dora was a sign that they'd found their pet. She'd be Dora II. They contacted the shelter and arranged for the adoption. A van would arrive at a predetermined Toronto location with their dog and various others that had been adopted. Brian and Geraldine could hardly wait.

> When we arrived there were other people like us excitedly waiting to pick up their new pets. But as the van pulled in and the shelter staff started to unload the dogs, there was a problem. There was no little Dora.

The mystery was solved when a car soon pulled in, carrying the littlest of the rescues—including Dora. To her new "parents" she was as a-dora-ble as her photo had shown.

It wasn't long before Brian and Geraldine realized that the newest member of their family had anxiety issues. She'd set off in a flurry of barking as soon as the doorbell rang and continue for several minutes. "It never matters if it's a stranger or someone who she's seen a dozen times before," says Geraldine. "She just goes nuts."

It soon became apparent that Dora had bigger issues than barking at callers. She began to have seizures. The couple's veterinarian diagnosed idiopathic epilepsy. For this she'd need twice-daily medication. The condition also caused a weakness in the dog's bladder. More medication for this, too.

"Our dogs have been my Mercedes," says Brian. "I'm sure our three dogs' health issues have, over the years, cost as much as a luxury car." Brian and Geraldine wouldn't have it any other way. "Our pets have brought us so much joy and pleasure; you can't put a price on that," says Brian.

XXX

And while Brian and Geraldine's hearts are fully captured by the canine members of their family, that's not to say other species get short shrift. The family pool and pool deck are testaments to this. A lattice contraption covers the steps leading into the pool. Brian explains:

> We knew that raccoons were getting inside the fence into our property because we'd seen them leaning into the pool to get a drink of water. Geraldine was horrified that one day she'd open the door to find a drowned raccoon.

So they had the barrier constructed, one which would prevent the raccoons from walking down the steps for water. The critters could still stand on the grate and safely stick their faces through to reach a drink. Even better, a ceramic pet dish filled daily with water invited them, as well as any passing squirrels, chipmunks or other wildlife, to quench their thirst.

Geraldine Williams' compassion for animals extends to stray cats too. She'd been aware of a strange cat in the neighbourhood, and from the look of it, the poor fellow had been in its fair share of scraps. A good meal had been a stranger for quite some time too. Geraldine took to leaving food outside for the homeless one. Brian continues the tale:

But it was cold out, so Geraldine started leaving the garage door open for the cat to come inside. Then she got some straw from a garden centre and built a manger so that it wouldn't freeze at night.

The naming of the cat as "Lucky" corresponded with its graduation to spending nights in the laundry room. No further though. "Brian's afraid of cats; he wanted nothing to do with him," offers Geraldine. Lucky was now getting medical attention too. Like every conscientious pet "owner," Geraldine had taken "her" cat to the veterinarian for vaccinations and neutering. It was here that she found out that she was not Lucky's only saviour.

> The vet asked me if I knew that another woman was also bringing him in for medical attention. And she called him "Zorro" because of his black mask. The vet said that it wasn't that unusual for feral cats to have more than one person looking out for them.

With this news, Geraldine took it upon herself to call on Lucky/ Zorro's other keeper—a woman in the same neighbourhood. The two pledged to share their cat's expenses in the future. But one day, Lucky/Zorro's good fortune ran out. He'd gone missing for several days and the next time Geraldine saw him, he was badly injured. "I imagine he'd been hit by a car because he was dragging his bad legs."

Geraldine and her cat-friend took him in for medical treatment. The vet thought they might be able to repair the damage, but ascertained that the cat would need weeks of inside nursing and attention. The two cat-rescuers had a decision to make.

Lucky was a street cat and who knows if he had ever been a house pet. We felt that it would be impossible to keep him locked up inside. So we made the hard decision to have him euthanized.

XXX

By now, Dora's anxiety has abated and she gives me a kiss before I leave. "But wait till I show you the buggy," says Brian, and he heads for the garage. It appears that Dora II loves her ride as much as Dora I did. On Brian's command—"Get in your buggy, Dora"—she hops in, and settles herself for an adventure. "Everybody in the neighbourhood knows us—and Dora—by now," chuckles Brian.

> Sometimes she walks and sometimes she wants to ride When she's walking, and we pass people in the street with our empty buggy, they will give us a look and often ask what's happened to the baby!

Looks don't bother Brian and Geraldine Williams at all. Anything for Dora!!!

LOVE!

Duke, Kuda and Mack

Yannick and Shantelle Bisson

Born in Montreal, Yannick Bisson, the star of CBC's hit series Murdoch Mysteries, has been acting since he was 13. His first break came at 15, when he acted in the CBC movie Hockey Night, starring Megan Follows and Rick Moranis. He then earned the lead role in the movie, Toby McTeague. More than 60 television and movie credits have followed including: Roxy Hunter, Casino Jack, Sue Thomas F.B.Eye, Flashpoint and Falcon Beach.

Stardom came when Yannick landed the role of Detective William Murdoch in the series "Murdoch Mysteries". An appealing combination of crime solving, romance and humour, spiced with a dash of Canadian history, "Murdoch Mysteries" is one of CBC's top-rated shows. As well, Yannick has branched into directing several episodes of the series.

Yannick's wife, Shantelle Bisson, is equally versatile, being an actress, writer and producer. The Bissons are parents to three daughters: Brianna, Dominique and Mikaela.

Protectors of the environment, with a belief in giving back to their community as well, Shantel and Yannick are supporters of Childhood Cancer Canada and Camp Oochigeas, which both support children with cancer.

The entire family calls themselves "dog crazy." Boxers and English Bulldogs are their breeds of choice.

xxx

As pet owners, Yannick and Shantelle Bisson take their roles seriously. In fact, they prefer the term "pet parents," or better still, "two-footed parents to our four-footed children." For the past several years, Boxer brothers Kuda and Mack, and an English Bulldog named Duke, have shared the Bissons' Toronto home. Yannick explains what pet parenting means to them:

> We've taken on the obligation of making our dogs integral parts of our family unit. They deserve no less than this. But we've also tried to teach them to be responsible canine citizens, in the house and in public. Dogs, like kids, need to behave in public so that they're not an annoyance or threat to people or other animals.

Providing top-notch medical care for their pets when they become sick is an integral part of the Bisson philosophy too. Shantelle, well read and an inveterate researcher in health matters, is the family expert in this area. She's been significantly challenged in her role during the past two years.

In the summer of 2011, Mack was diagnosed with a mast cell tumour on his thigh. The diagnosis came as a blow but it was not unexpected. Shantelle explains: "We knew that, as a breed, Boxers were prone to this cancer. But we were still devastated when it appeared. Mast cell tumours are so aggressive and unpredictable."

At the time, only five years old, Mack was given four to six months to live. The family decided to meet the diagnosis head on. With Shantelle taking the lead, they'd summon up every known support and strategy—through both conventional medicine and alternative therapy.

They'd first trust the deep medical knowledge and skills of their veterinarian, Dr. Matthew Croskery, at the Oak Park Animal Hospital in Oakville. "Dr. Matt" began treatment by surgically removing Mack's tumour. Close post-surgical care followed.

Then, Dr. Victoria Dale-Harris of Toronto, "Vici", a veterinarian and doctor of naturopathic medicine, stepped in to play her part. According to Shantelle, various treatments and supplements were meant to build up Mack's immune system. "Dr. Vici" cautioned the family: "I cannot guarantee you anything, but I will promise to do everything I can." She'd return to the Bisson home every six weeks to re-evaluate Mack's progress.

xxx

Daily walks in the ravine and lots of play supplemented Mack's medical therapy. But there was one additional step that the Bissons took in their fight against Mack's cancer.

Both Bissons are committed environmentalists. They had been in the process of building a new "green" home when Mack became ill. They now decided to incorporate elements to make it a "clean" home too: "Not just for our dogs, but for our daughters and ourselves," Shantelle explains.

> We researched and found recycled products to be used as floors, and paints with no VOCs [Volatile Organic Com pounds]. And we brought in cabinets and furniture that were either locally made or with low-to-zero VOCs. Yannick even went so far as to hire an electro-magnetic sensitive electrician specialist. He created an electrical plan that ensured that none of the wiring in the house would create fields of electro-magnetic currents. We also had the home wired with BX cable to further ensure safe sleeping zones around all bedrooms and the dogs' sleeping zones.

xxx

The Bisson family strongly believes in the power of emotional support in times of trouble, so they surrounded their boy with as much positive energy as they could muster. Shantelle recalls their "pep talks."

> We'd hold his face and look Mack in the eye and say to him: "We are working as hard as we can to save you, Boy, and you have to do your part. You've got to be strong and fight this cancer. You're not allowed to die."

The movie The Bucket List also provided part of their healing therapy. In the film, two dying men decide to fulfill their dreams before they die. This carpe diem philosophy inspired Yannick and Shantelle to create a bucket list for Mack. Top of the list was an acting job in Yannick's Murdoch Mysteries.

In October 2011, Mack went to work with his dad. They were filming the Season 5, Episode 12 of the series called "Murdoch Night in Canada." Prime Minister Stephen Harper, a fan of the show, had a hand in suggesting the plot line of the episode. In the concluding scene, Murdoch and his colleagues at Police Station Number 4 engage in a friendly game of street hockey. Watching the game from the sidelines is a handsome Boxer.

During the filming, Yannick regularly updated Shantelle from his cell phone on Mack's acting debut. "We took his collar off and he didn't leave my side, even though there were horses and dozens of new people for him to meet," Yannick reported.

Mack never needed to go past Number 1 on his bucket List. A body scan done two months after therapy showed no tumours. His energy and spirits were high too. "It was when he took a flying leap over the couch that we knew he was feeling great," laughs Yannick. Dr. Matt joined Dr. Vici in being cautiously optimistic at Mack's prognosis. Shantelle recalls the words she had prayed to hear. "Dr. Matt told us: "Well, it's clear that Mack is not going to die in the four-to-six-month period we'd first predicted. I won't guarantee he'll live to age 14, but he won't be dying in the near future."

The labour of love that Yannick and Shantelle Bisson had undertaken has brought shining results. Two years after Mack's brush with death, he remains strong and vital.

xxx

But in May 2013, a black cloud appeared in the skies. In the late spring, Kuda, Mack's brother, lost some weight and wasn't his usual gregarious self. A visit to Dr. Matt and an ultrasound showed he too had developed a mast cell tumour. Kuda's prognosis was far worse than Mack's had been two years before. Kuda was given one to two weeks (with no treatment) to live.

Stunned by the diagnosis, as well as the short window of life, the family agreed that only the "heavy artillery" of chemotherapy would give their beloved Kuda a chance to live. He'd begin the therapy immediately. At the same time, Dr. Vici would try to work her "magic." Yannick expresses the emotional toll that their pets' cancer has taken on him.

> Losing pets is so, so painful. It just rips me apart—so much so that at times I just can't bear the thoughts of doing it again. And I think that maybe it's better not to have pets, so we... don't have to go through this loss.

He smiles sadly: "But my women always talk me into another pet. I agree and I'm drawn in again. What are you going to do?"

Author's note: Kuda passed away in the summer of 2013.

El Chompa, "The Bushbaby," Gossie and Smallwood

Robert Bateman

Born in Toronto in 1930, Robert Bateman was a precociously artistic child. He drew and sketched from an early age, with animals being his subjects of preference. But art was something he did for fun—not for a career. Teaching was. From 1955 to 1976, he taught high school Art and Geography, taking a two-year sabbatical to teach in Nigeria, Africa.

The experience would prove pivotal to his artistic future when he began selling his art through a Nairobi art dealer. In 1976, he left teaching to devote himself full-time to painting. The world of nature and the animal world of Canada and beyond came under the skilled Bateman brush.

By the late 1970's, Robert Bateman's work was achieving unparalleled recognition in Canada and internationally. His one-man exhibition at the Smithsonian Institution in Washington drew record crowds for any artist's work.

He's been the subject of a number of films, including ones produced for the CBC and the National Film Board.

In 1985, he moved to Salt Spring Island, British Columbia. Now 83, he continues to paint. A dog lover, he is currently without pets.

xxx

Since he first put paint to canvas over seven decades ago, nature and the creatures within it have defined the art of Robert Bateman. A Canadian resident for most of his 83 years, still, Bob has not let geography limit his landscape.

Lions from the African savannah; snow leopards of the Asian mountains; giant pandas from the remote mountains of China; and toucans from the South American rainforests have vividly come to life thanks to the precise and delicate Bateman brushstrokes.

An observer and admirer of domestic animals too, Bob has also celebrated his dogs on canvas. Labrador Retrievers have been a particular favourite. His beloved dog Smallwood, whom he described as "mostly a Labrador Retriever but his grandmother was a Newfoundland" and named for the first premier of Newfoundland, was the subject of a number of Bateman canvases.

One of Bateman's best-known works, titled "Artist and His Dog" sees the two on a countryside hike. Both are positioned in the background, to the right of a spreading pine. They're shrouded in mist. In the distinct foreground, a field of yellow grass with two spiky goldenrods poke their heads above the foliage. In explaining his choice of muting human and animal to emphasize vegetation, Bob explains:

> Smallwood's enthusiasm and interest in the landscape were always inspiring. I found myself noticing things that he noticed. In this painting, I have elaborated on a complex jumble of meadow plants, which would be at the level of Smallwood's world.

He has sheltered creatures of the wild too. Three of his most unforgettable ones came to him on foreign adventures.

xxx

A Mexican coatimundi entered Robert Bateman's world in 1955

when he and his brother were on an extended trip to Mexico to photograph exotic birds. Coatimundis are members of the raccoon family. They weigh between 4 and 6 kilograms, with their length being around 100 centimetres. Half of that is their prodigious ringed tail.

Coatis are highly inquisitive and social, needing company around them to be content. They like humans and will often attach themselves to them. Sometimes to their peril. This had been the case when Bob and his brother found one helpless animal.

> We had come across a bunch of local kids who had captured a baby coatimundi and were swinging it around by its long tail. They were torturing it and we had to step in to save it. So we bought it from them.

Not sure what they had gotten themselves into once they had the animal secure, the brothers didn't worry for long.

> The baby quickly imprinted on us as part of his family and was easily tamed. We called him El Chompa because he would eat anything we ate. And when it was time for us to go to sleep he insisted on sleeping with one of us in our sleeping bag. Before he settled down, he'd inspect our hair thoroughly and then go on searching for non-existent scorpions in our ears. Finally, after tickling our ribs, he'd end up as a muff around our neck.

Needless to say, one brother would try to pass Chompa on to the other to "babysit" at nighttime! Nor was all the activity at nighttime. Daytime climbing was a favourite activity. "Chompa loved to climb and would go straight up our body into our arms when we were trying to eat lunch. His mission was to intercept our sandwiches."

When the boys set out on their photographic expeditions, the faithful coati would tag along. "He'd try to walk between our feet, thinking they were his brothers, because they were about his size." Bob recalls that the feeling of "brotherhood" between them and their faithful coatimundi was mutual.

The memories of his dearly beloved coati almost 60 years ago still tug at Robert Bateman's heartstrings. "Even recalling him now makes me teary-eyed. He really had become a part of our little extended family during out Mexican safari."

xxx

Bob learned a lot about African wildlife during his two-year teaching stint in Nigeria. He'd always been the observer in the field and he did a fair amount of that. But a couple of exotic species lived under his roof as pets during his Nigerian stay. So he had the opportunity to come to know these species more intimately.

One was a Demidoff's galago, a member of the bushbaby family and one of the world's most diminutive primates. "This guy was so small, he could fit into a tea cup," recalls Bob. In contrast to their tiny bodies, Demidoffs have huge eyes and enormous ears, which can turn independently of each other. The better to listen for the insects they prey upon.

The creature's eating etiquette was exact.

> He'd sleep all day and come out in the evening to be fed. His diet consisted of grasshoppers plus milk and honey. Grasshoppers he'd always seize vertically like you would an ice cream. Then he'd eat them from the head down. The milk and honey we fed to him by spoon.

Full of energy too, the Demidoff enjoyed time out of his cage.

> He'd bounce around the living room from the picture frames to the lampshades onto my head and neck. I'd notice that the pads of his feet seemed sticky and wondered why. Then I learned that they urinate on their hands and feet to leave a scent trail back to their nest after foraging all night in the forest. That accounted for the stickiness.

xxx

A highly social dwarf mongoose named Gossie was another Nigerian companion pet. Approximately the size of a human foot, the mongoose had a long snout, pointy ears and dark brown fur. Gossie was a gregarious companion who bonded with his human quickly and deeply. "He liked to nestle in my lap when I sat down, just like a house cat," Bob reminisces.

But Gossie's need to be close could be annoying too. "He'd walk between my legs, getting me all tangled up with him. I had to be careful I didn't step on him, because he was so small I could have crushed him."

> But lap-sitting was where Gossie's cat characteristics ended. He was more doglike in his responsiveness and he came when he was called. Smart too. He even housetrained himself without being taught.

And like a dog, Gossie liked to fetch. But his rules were a bit different than the usual "human throws dog the stick, and dog runs and fetches it."

> Gossie did his fetch game independently and with a different sort of ball. His was the top of a ball point pen. He'd carry the top to one side of the living room, which had a slippery concrete floor. He'd then face the wall and snap the plastic top between his legs like in a real football game. Then he'd chase the spinning top across the floor, grab it and growl.

Bob compares the relationship between this out-of-the-ordinary pet and the more traditional human–dog bond.

> Our emotional attachment to dogs is very strong, but in some ways the bond I had with my mongoose was stronger. He was self-taught in coming when he was called, in house-training himself and in the fetch-it game.

XXX

Smallwood, the Labrador Retriever, was Robert Bateman's last pet. "I travel so much now, it's not right to keep one," he explains. His excursions around the globe to photograph and then paint wildlife will have to do, he explains. "Still, it makes me sad. I do miss my dogs."

LOVE!

Freddy and Jazzy

Shaun Majumder

Raised in the tiny town of Burlington, on Newfoundland's west coast, Shaun Majumder seemed destined for show business. He could make people laugh, and he did so routinely. He was, after all, a Newfoundlander, geographically disposed to see the funny side of life.

Shaun got his start in show business performing in school concerts and plays. He then moved to Ontario where he secured his first job as an announcer for the YTV children's game show "CLIPS". Gigs as a host of the kids show "Brain Wash" and the popular game show "Uh Oh!" followed.

The CBC show "This Hour Has 22 Minutes" followed in 2003. Here Shaun immortalized a number of his alter egos, including Raj Binder, the sweaty and bumbling TV reporter.

On "22 Minutes", Shaun's comedic star rose steadily. He went on to host three seasons of the "Just for Laughs" comedy series. He also appeared in Mary Walsh's series «Hatching, Matching and Dispatching".

Shaun's break into U.S. television came when he starred in "Cedric the Entertainer Presents". This was followed by the short-lived comedy "Unhitched". His career took a dramatic turn when he was cast in several episodes of the hit series "24" with Kiefer Sutherland. This led to starring roles in the critically acclaimed ABC cop drama "Detroit 187", then the NC legal drama "The Firm".

Shaun still remained attached to Newfoundland, especially Burlington. He was looking to do something to contribute to his hometown's economy. Thus, "Majumder Manor" was born. The reality show followed Shaun's efforts to build a small hotel in Burlington. Various family, friends and members of the community were featured in the show.

Shaun now spends his time in Newfoundland, Halifax, where "22 Minutes" is filmed, and Los Angeles. He and his wife, actress Shelby Fenner, share their lives with two Boston Terriers, Freddy and Jasmine Beauchamps, known as Jazzy.

xxx

Shaun Majumder states right off the bat that when he moved to Los Angeles he had no immediate intention of being a dog owner. He loved dogs and had them as a kid, but as a peripatetic entertainer, with one foot in East Coast Canada and the other in the American West Coast, he felt too nomadic to bring a dog into his life.

His wife, Shelby Fenner, loved dogs too. A friend had a lovely Boston Terrier named Jasmine Beauchamps, Jazzy for short. Every time Shelby went to visit, her fondness for the breed grew. The Boston is known in dog circles as "the American Gentleman," for its neat black and white coat, resembling a tuxedo. Its personable nature wins points too.

Shelby told Shaun about the dog, and wondered about owning one.

> With me gone so often, and Shelby alone in a house in the northeast side of Los Angeles, she thought having a dog for protection might be a good idea. So her friend offered to let her borrow Jazzy for a week or so. Since I wasn't that keen on the idea, the temporary situation was ideal.

So, Jazzy came to vacation with Shelby while Shaun was in Canada. It was a win-win situation for both human and dog. Compared to her permanent home on the seventh floor of an apartment building, Jazzy found Shaun and Shelby's house, with a real backyard, to be like heaven.

Still a few days before Shaun's return, Shelby made plans to return Jazzy to her owner. Her friend's response was music to Shelby's ears.

> He suggested that we keep Jazzy for as long as we wanted—knowing that his dog would be better off with us than with him in his cramped little apartment. Shelby wanted to keep her forever but the waters would be tested once I got home.

Shaun took at least seven days to fall head over heels in love with the charming Jazzy. No surprise, given the Boston's Terrier's reputation as an outgoing, eager to please, intelligent and easily trained canine. The breed is not given to excessive barking or needing lots of exercise. Protective of their owners despite their diminutive size, the Boston is thought by their owners to be "perfect companions."

Still, Shaun remembers this interlude as a stressful time.

> As soon as I felt that superbond starting to take between Jazzy and me, I knew that she had to go back home right away or not at all. I couldn't take bonding with her anymore if I was to lose her. Then Shelby told me the situation with her friend—that she was ours if I wanted her. Needless to say, if wasn't hard for me to say yes. We were keeping this dog—forever.

XXX

In the shake of a tail, Jazzy Majumder became a media darling. She hosts her own Twitter page @jazziejumder. "I'm a Boston Terrier livin' in L.A., loving the Burl in Nfld & hangin' with Shelby and Whazzisname Majumder," she tweets.

Jazzy also has starred on a delightful YouTube video called "Jazzy

Listens." With the sound of a mewing kitten in the background, Jazzy turns her head this way and that way, cocking her ears to the left and right to hone in on the mysterious sound. "I just want to chase the sound but don't know where it is coming from" is the tagline.

And if Jazzy wasn't famous enough, a photo of Shaun holding his #1 pooch—both wearing similar facial expressions was chosen as one of the Toronto Globe and Mail's top photos of 2012.

XXX

Jazzy's "livin' in the big city" dog role had a makeover during the filming of Shaun's 2013 CBC series Majumder Manor. During the shooting period, Shelby and Jazzy were frequent visitors to little Burlington, Newfoundland.

One of the show's episodes showed Jazzy, outfitted in her own day-glo lifejacket, taking her first ride in a motorboat. True to her "I wanna try it too" personality, she's having a blast, feet planted on the side of the Zodiac, in the bracing Newfoundland sea air.

Another saw Jazzy and Shelby out on a fishing rig cod-jigging.

XXX

One day Shelby looked out the window of her L.A. house and saw Jazzy peeing on their lawn furniture. She shouted "Jazzy stop that" and the dog disappeared from sight. But it seemed that Jazzy was presently sleeping on the couch with Shaun! There was a Jazzy doppelganger on the loose in the neighbourhoood.

Concerned for the dog's welfare in what Shaun calls a "coyote-infested area," the couple got in the car and started searching. There were no sightings of a Jazzy lookalike until a week later when Shelby was out driving. She saw the Jazzy-clone and stopped. "And the dog hopped right into her car," Shaun laughs.

Further investigating found that the Boston, a male but older than Jazzy from its' grey-flecked face, did have an owner who lived in the neighbourhood. "But I guess the dog was a bit of an escape artist and was living more on the streets than anywhere else," says Shaun.

When Shaun went to take the dog back where he belonged, there didn't seem much interest on either side of reuniting. And so Freddy, a six-year old male, became part of the Majumder–Fenner household—a big brother for Jazzy.

Given his free-and-easy lifestyle, Freddy had some behavioural issues, the most worrisome being a nasty aggression towards the smaller Jazzy. "He was a gangster dog at first," says Shaun. No small wonder, for a little guy virtually on his own in the world.

He'd never been trained to walk on a leash either. But in time, with Shelby and Shaun's love, a fair amount of behavioural training, mixed with the security of living in a real home, Freddy became a calmer and kinder dog.

The result is shown in Shaun's YouTube video called "Happy Dogs." The two dogs tussle amicably with a rope on a grassy bank in Burlington, Newfoundland.

When Shaun and Shelby take the dogs through American Customs, the officials invariably want to see the dogs out of their travelling cases. Shaun is happy to oblige. "So while the guards are making a big fuss about my dogs on the conveyor belt, I can smuggle all that Tim Hortons coffee and no one notices," he jokes.

Both Jazzy and Freddy will be featured in episodes of Majumder Manor, Season 2, in the summer of 2014.

XXX

"So I never really went out to get myself a dog—or two," laughs Shaun. "They just kind of happened." Nevertheless both Shaun and

Shelby are head over heels in love with their furry family.

"Boston Terriers are the perfect dog," Shaun says. "And I can't see myself ever wanting another breed. These guys are playful, smart and have a big personality."

"And," says the man who was judged Canada's funniest comedian, "they've got a great sense of humour too."

LOVE!

Galileo, Pooky and Whiskey

David Mirvish

The words "entertainment mogul" only scratch the surface of David Mirvish's multi-faceted public face. As the owner of Toronto's Royal Alexandra Theatre, the Princess of Wales Theatre, the Ed Mirvish Theatre and the Panasonic Theatre, as well as past owner of London's legendary Old Vic Theatre, David adds "bookstore and art gallery" proprietor, as well as real estate developer to his impressive life portfolio.

In 1987, he and his father, Ed, founded Mirvish Productions, with the aim of bringing the best of live performing to Canadian audiences. Over the succeeding decades, Mirvish Productions has brought hits such as "Miss Saigon", "The Lion King", "Les Misérables", "Tommy", "Mama Mia" and "Hairspray" to sold-out Toronto audiences.

David has given back to his beloved city too, serving as a member of the board of trustees of the Royal Ontario Museum and the National Gallery of Canada. In 2012, he was named chancellor of the University of Guelph.

But it's his role as art collector that brings the real twinkle to David Mirvish's eyes. Since the early 1960's, he's been a savvy connoisseur of the most luminous of European and North American abstract expressionist canvases.

In 2012, he entered into an ambitious partnership with architect Frank Gehry. The two began plans to house the extensive Mirvish art collection in a public gallery within a proposed new high-rise housing development in the King Street West area of Toronto. Mr. Mirvish envisions the building as looking like "sculptures that people would live in."

David Mirvish lives in Toronto with his wife, Audrey, and his dog, Galileo Figaro.

XXX

David Mirvish's stories about the pets that have been a part of his life are often tinged with humour—and nostalgia. He recalls his first dog, a Dalmatian that his father brought home for him when he was a child. "It was a beautiful creature, but wild. The first time we left him alone he proceeded to try to chew the leg off our dining room table."

With a laugh, David notes that his dad preferred having a sit-down place to eat his dinner, over the idea of having a dog. So a new home was found for the spotted "Jaws."

The late Anne Mirvish, David's mother who had grown up with dogs, had a softer spot in her heart for puppy antics. She adored Whiskey, the family's next dog. Alas! Whiskey got into the odd piece of household mischief too. "Dad just felt dogs were too destructive and so Whiskey went to live with my grandmother," recalls David.

XXX

David's childhood memories of dog ownership weren't dark enough to preclude him from being a dog guardian as an adult. "I'm great at petting them; my wife, Audrey, is much better at feeding them and looking after them," he chuckles. And so dogs with names such as Marigold, Basil and Pooky played their parts in his grown-up life.

Committed to being responsible pet owners, Audrey and David always enrolled the family pooch in dog obedience classes. The exercise seemed to come with mixed results. Take Pooky, the white French Bulldog.

> Pooky just couldn't seem to get the hang of walking on a leash. He'd lag behind most of the time, and then when he would decide to keep up with you, he'd be distracted by a smell he'd tracked down under a bush. It was impossible to take that dog for a stroll.

One day Pooky escaped from the Mirvish house and found himself under the wheels of a car on the street. David and Audrey ran out to the street thinking the worst. "Pooky had survived without a scratch. His coat just carried the impression of the tire treads for a while," David remembers.

David and Audrey's current family pet is Galileo, a gift from their daughter, Hannah. The dog arrived already christened. "I thought at first she'd named him after the astronomer, but it turns out I was wrong. He's named after...." David forgets the reference and searches for a few minutes till it comes to him. "I've got it. It's a name in the song 'Bohemian Rhapsody' by the British group Queen. I better remember it. I produced the show!"

One of Galileo's chief jobs, with his owner, was to visit David's mother. Incapacitated for a number of years, Anne Mirvish lived in her own home, close to David and Audrey. She passed away on September 20, 2013, at the age of 94. David and Galileo's visits to Anne were a labour of love—one which they tried to follow every evening. "The dog just brought so much joy to my mother," says David.

> Her eyes would just light up when we came in. And always Galileo would come over to her and she'd pet him. He always gave her a kiss and licks on her hand. She loved that, and found his presence so soothing.

With Galileo now entering his own senior years, age 11, David knows his pet's time is short. And this brings him sadness.

> It's so emotionally hard to lose a dog you have loved and has meant so much to you. You become emotionally attached to

> them and then they leave you—they're gone. That's just bad manners!

From memories of a dog that ate a dining room table, to delight in one that brought unbridled joy to a dear family member, David Mirvish's dogs have been a constant in his own rich and giving life. He suggests that medical science should be doing more to increase the lifespan of household pets.

> I wonder why dogs' lives are still so short. You know I read in the paper the other day that medical science predicts that soon people will be living up to one hundred and fifty years. Now, why can't scientists do something to let the animals we love live longer?

Why can't they indeed?

LOVE!

Gentle Ben, Jasper, Simmy and Tilly

George and Susan Cohon

George Cohon's accomplishments go far beyond the fast-food business. American-born and educated, he practised law in Chicago. Then In 1967, George, his wife, Susan, and their young family headed north of the border. George had been given an assignment.

He'd become the franchisee charged with the task of expanding McDonald's in Canada. Four years later, in 1971, George Cohon became chairman, president and chief executive officer of McDonald's Restaurants of Canada. He and Susan became Canadian citizens in 1975.

George also spearheaded the introduction of McDonald's to the Soviet Union. In 1990, the biggest restaurant of the chain was opened in Moscow.

A humanitarian too, George founded Ronald McDonald House Charities in Canada. The 14 Canadian Ronald McDonald Houses provide accommodation for families whose children are receiving medical treatment at nearby hospitals.

George and Susan Cohon are long-time dog-guardians. Golden Retrievers, whom George names "the most loving, non-judgmental dogs in the world," are their breed of choice.

xxx

"The funny thing is that George used to be afraid of dogs," laughs Susan Cohon. "But that all changed when we got Jasper." The gregarious George suggests: "Let me tell you the story of how it all started."

> After our son Mark celebrated his Bar Mitzvah, our friend Fred Turner asked him how much money he had received. Fred told Mark that he should take at least half of it and invest it—"for your future," Fred said. Then Fred recommended a "great stock." So Mark followed Fred's advice, and eventually lost all of his investment when the stock crashed.

The well-meaning Turner felt bad about the "bad steer," and promptly bought the younger Cohon a Golden Retriever pup to make amends. And so dogs entered the Cohon family's life. What they didn't know about the Golden ball of love was that Jasper had been born in a puppy mill. "So he was a sick dog from day one," says George.

A myriad of health problems plagued the unfortunate Jasper, including cancer. It was through searching for quality care for their beloved dog's health problems that the Cohons heard of the exceptional work in cancer treatment that was going on at the Ontario Veterinary College at the University of Guelph.

"Guelph saved Jasper's life and for that we are forever grateful to them," states George. After cancer treatment, Jasper had what George calls "a good long life."

xxx

Phoenix followed Jasper and he too led the life of Riley in the Cohon house. But as comes all too soon for our canine friends, he too passed. George and Susan had opposite takes on getting a new dog. "I was like, 'let's take some time to mourn Phoenix's loss,' says Susan. George was 'we gotta get another dog right away!'"

They'd heard of Sherri Hall, a well-respected breeder of Golden Retrievers in Alliston, Ontario, and visited her kennels, Maplelane

Goldens. Predictably the Cohons returned home with a pup. He was Gentle Ben, an eight-month-old male. Ben was a sweetheart; but country-born and raised, he wasn't accustomed to the noise of a big city.

"So taking a big dog for a walk when he wants to turn back home was no easy matter," says Susan. Eventually they decided that Gentle Ben was not the dog for them and made a return journey to Alliston. They left with Tilly, a six-year-old female, retired as a breeding dog.

Calm, gentle and nurturing, Tilly would add another dimension to George and Susan Cohon's lives.

xxx

George Cohon calls himself a "hands-on guy." "I never just give money to good causes; I always like to get involved too," he acknowledges. Through his and Susan's work at Ronald McDonald House, where illness and worry often dominate the daily mood, they were aware how the soft touch and warm muzzle of a visiting therapy dog was often the best medicine.

"And we knew that with Tilly's nature, she would make an outstanding therapy dog," says George. After completing the requisite training through the Delta Society Therapy Dogs, George and Susan, with Tilly in tow, began making regular rounds at Toronto's Baycrest Hospital and Ronald McDonald House. Baycrest specializes in geriatric and palliative care, while Ronald McDonald House directs its attention towards seriously ill children and their families.

From her first visit to Baycrest, intuitively Tilly knew why she was visiting. "She'd gently place her head on a lap or on the person's bed. And they'd always reach out their hand to pet her," offers George. They soon found that even with people weighed down so heavily with illness, Tilly's presence was the spark that would open them to smiles and conversation.

> They'd start talking about a dog they had when they were younger. All the time, they'd be petting Tilly who'd sit peacefully and patiently beside them. Tilly just has that special quality of making people happy. She is amazing.

George recalls a conversation he had with a Baycrest patient, only in her fifties but dying of cancer. One day when one of the woman's oncologists saw the effect that Tilly had on his patient, he asked George and Susan to bring the dog to visit her as often as possible. "Tilly does more good for her than anything else," observed the doctor.

XXX

Sometime later, Simmy, one of Tilly's pups, became a member of the Cohon home. Naturally, she joined her mom on the Cohon therapy dog team. Since then, the sight of these two magnificent Golden Retrievers has never failed to bring a light to peoples' eyes. "And when we tell them they're mother and daughter, then people are even more thrilled to make their acquaintance," says George.

The patients loved to hear stories that George and Susan would tell about the dogs too. George remembers fondly the effect that a story about Simmy had on a patient who had not spoken for some days.

> I felt she could hear me, even if she didn't respond so I started to tell her about Simmy, who had swiped an entire loaf of bread off the counter, opened the plastic, eaten all the bread and left the plastic wrapper behind. I finished the story and the woman smiled, looked at Simmy and said: "Simmy you are a bad dog!"

"That's the kind of therapy that dogs like these two can bring," George says, proudly.

In addition to the satisfaction that Susan gains knowing how much her dogs have meant to the people in need, she also finds the visits stimulating. "I learn so much talking to the people I meet on our therapy dog rounds—people from other cultures; people who have had fascinating lives."

xxx

Now that George is no longer CEO of McDonald's Canada, he and Susan have become snowbirds. They now retire to their Florida home each winter. Of course, the dogs come with them and go to work in the south.

They visit residents of a nearby palliative care facility. It seems the dogs' Canadian magic works just as well in Florida. George summarizes why his dogs are so effective in their therapy.

> They are totally non-judgmental and these two dogs just love everyone. They treat everyone the same—no matter their age, racial background or income. The good that Tilly and Simmy do just can't be measured.

xxx

George adds a touching postscript to the story of Gentle Ben. After he returned to Alliston, the big guy found his niche as one of the therapy dogs in the C.O.P.E. program. C.O.P.E. Service Dogs, founded by Jane Noake of Barrie, aim to improve the lives of the disabled, or at-risk youth or those struggling at school. The elderly are served too.

C.O.P.E.'s "Canines in the Classroom" program teaches at-risk high school students to be dog trainers, at the same time giving them leadership and employment skills. Gentle Ben was matched with a young girl named Krysta and became an integral part of her development. The Cohons are honorary patrons of C.O.P.E.

Henry

Liisa Winkler

Growing up long and lean, in her hometown of Belleville, Ontario, Liisa Winkler seemed destined to become a dancer. With this goal in mind, she attended the respected Quinte Ballet School of Canada in Belleville.

But then one day in 1993, out shopping with her mom, she was spotted by a modelling agent. Before she could say "Vogue," 15-year-old Liisa Winkler found herself a high fashion model.

"I'd grown far too tall to be a professional dancer anyway," states Liisa. But her 5 foot 11 inch height and angular frame made her a modelling commodity worldwide, and her star rose meteorically. She appeared on the covers of "Vogue", "Harper's Bazaar", "Elle", "Marie Claire", "Allure", "Glamour" and "Flare" & "Fashion Magazine".

A darling of the runway too, Liisa travelled the world wearing the designs of Gucci, Calvin Klein, Ralph Lauren, Valentino, Versace and Armani, to name a few.

But there is much more to Liisa Winkler than a pretty face. Over the years, she's been a supporter of the David Suzuki Foundation, the World Society for the Protection of Animals (WSPA), and the Farm Sanctuary, which advocates for farm animals.

Liisa is married to Ryan Boorne, retired principal dancer of the National Ballet Company. They live in Toronto with their two young children, Stella, seven, and Oskar, four, as well as their well-adored Labradoodle, Henry.

xxx

One of the first things that Liisa Winkler and Ryan Boorne did when they bought their first house in 2010 was to get a dog. Liisa had grown up with Labrador Retrievers and she felt they were "the only dog to have."

But living in the city with a modest backyard, they readjusted their sights towards a more diminutive breed. As they had children they also wanted to make sure that the pet they brought into their lives would be genetically kid-friendly.

And so Henry, a female mini-Labradoodle came home to stay. She immediately bonded with Ryan, who, having retired from the National Ballet Company of Canada, often held down the "fort" while Liisa travelled for fashion shoots and premieres.

Henry viewed Ryan as "the leader of her pack," says Liisa.

> But their bond was more than that. Henry seemed to sense if Ryan was stressed or something was bothering him. He might not even be showing anything, but Henry would know. She'd go over to him and put her head on his lap, as if to say "I'm here for you."

On the rare occasion that Ryan needed to be away for some time and Liisa was at home, Henry became stressed.

xxx

Unlike many family dogs who characteristically steer clear of noisy and unpredictable children, Henry immediately adored young Stella, Liisa and Ryan's first child. And Stella grew to adore Henry right back.

> Henry didn't mind Stella dressing her up in doll clothes and generally treating her as if she were Stella's doll. Stella would hug her and kiss her and Henry was always tolerant.

But if Stella got a bit rough in her play, Henry had her own way of teaching her little friend to be gentle. "She'd give Stella gentle swats of the paw or nips," says Liisa. "Kids seem to like pulling on fur, but Stella learned not to do this, thanks to Henry's gentle teaching." Liisa viewed this teaching as "a very mothering thing for Henry to do—she treated Stella as if she were one of her puppies!"

The extent of the bond between Stella and Henry became vividly apparent when, one day, Stella was jumping on the living room couch and fell off, injuring her arm. Henry came running when she heard her little friend's cries.

> Ryan and I comforted Stella, but thought maybe she was just being a bit dramatic, because the arm looked fine. But Henry continued to whimper and lick Stella, sitting on her stomach and howling, which was a sound that Henry had never made before. It was like she was telling us to look again.

Liisa and Ryan decided to act on what their dog seemed to be telling them. And as it turned out, Stella had fractured her arm.

Ryan and Liisa were astounded by their dog's intuitiveness. "How did Henry know that there was really something wrong with Stella? Could she smell something? Was there a difference in Stella's cry?" Liisa ponders.

From this point on, the household paid more attention to Henry's reactions.

xxx

As Stella has grown, the bond between the little girl and her dog has changed. Now the seven-year-old looks to Henry as a confidant. "When Stella is sad, she will lie beside Henry and tell her her troubles. I think it truly makes Stella feel better."

The bond between Oskar and Henry took longer to develop. But now at age four, Oskar has become more significant to Henry. "Henry likes to sit on Oskar's bed while we read him stories and tuck him in. Then she leaves when he is quiet," says Liisa.

The protective side of Henry's behaviour was seen when Liisa took Henry along when walking her children to school. But if either Stella or Oskar stopped to pay attention to another dog on the sidewalk, Henry reacted. "She would actually stand between the kids and the other dog, sometimes even emitting a low growl," reports Liisa. Henry now remains at home for walk-to-school-time.

The ultimate Henry ritual in the Boorne/Winkler household is bedtime. Usual lights out for Liisa and Ryan is ten-ish, and Henry will wait on the landing until they come upstairs. Before turning in, Liisa will go into her children's rooms to make sure all is well.

> If I'm delayed going into the kids' rooms, Henry will become impatient and come in to see what I am doing, or she'll whine. Henry is not satisfied until I am done my checking and head back to our own bedroom. She'll then lie down to sleep for the night.

On the rare occasion when Henry is distracted by another "urgent dogly matter" and misses Liisa's checking on the kids, she'll alert Liisa. "I often have to pretend to check them again just to get her to go to sleep!"

xxx

Caring for her own dog to the very best of her ability is just part of Liisa Winkler's work to make the world a better place for animals.

She lends her time as "celebrity ambassador" with WSPA (World Society for the Protection of Animals). Her attention is primarily paid to the treatment of farm animals.

She also writes a blog for WSPA's "Choose Cage Free" website. In this connection she visits "happy hens" in the country and is working on a video project to help raise awareness to improve the life for caged farm animals. Liisa also is part of WSPA's Collars Not Cruelty campaign to help vaccinate dogs.

There's never an age too young to make kids aware of animal welfare issues, says Liisa. She and Ryan have incorporated this into their "home teachings." They plan to adopt a shelter dog or two when Stella and Oskar are a little older: Liisa explained "So they'll be able to see how they can make a difference in an animal's life."

For the present, "Henry has played a large part in shaping both Stella and Oskar into the caring animal lovers they are today." Like parents, like children.

The Istanbul Street Cat and Pancake

Graeme Smith

A New Hamburg, Ontario, native, Graeme Smith was hired as a news correspondent by the Globe and Mail after graduation from the Journalism Program at Ryerson University. He was later promoted to be the paper's Moscow correspondent. In 2006, he took on the gruelling role of Afghanistan correspondent.

Graeme's reports from Kandahar were characterized as telling the "human aspects of war." He brought to light the physical abuses by Afghan authorities on Afghan prisoners of war—and the Canadian Forces' complicity in this.

In 2007, he was awarded the National Newspaper Award, Canada's highest award for print journalism, and a Michener Award for public service. His later multi-part series of newspaper and online articles, "Talking to the Taliban" won him 2009's Emmy Award for "Best New Approaches to News and Documentary."

A year of book writing about his Afghanistan experiences followed, before he moved on to Delhi, India, as the Globe's South Asia correspondent. Then in 2011, it was to Istanbul as a roving reporter.

In December 2012, he left the Globe to become Senior Analyst at Crisis Group International. Crisis Group is a non-profit, non-governmental organization that conducts research and produces reports on zones of conflict around the world.

His book "The Dogs Are Eating Them Now: Our War in Afghanistan" was published in September 2013 and won the Hilary Weston Writers' Trust Prize for Nonfiction.

An admirer and protector of cats, Graeme has a firm belief that these creatures find their humans, not the other way around.

xxx

Graeme Smith's cat theory was tested in 2011, during his time in Istanbul. Returning to his apartment, he was startled to witness a cat appear from the stairwell. It dashed inside his apartment ahead of him.

> I had to climb several flights of an old stairway to get to my place, so it wasn't an everyday occurrence to find a cat waiting for me. In this part of the world, at least, street cats aren't usually so bold.

Graeme soon learned the reason for this one's urgency.

> It was a female cat, pregnant, and she was looking for a quiet place to give birth. Once inside the door, she immediately disappeared behind a heavy clothes dresser in my bedroom. I gave her some food and let her be.

Graeme's houseguest eventually gave birth to a single kitten. "I knew enough about cats to realize that this meant that she was either very young, or malnourished, or both." In any case, it looked like Mama and baby were there to stay.

> I took care of them, and watched the baby kitten grow into a frisky little animal with incredibly sharp claws. It enjoyed climbing me from foot to head, using these tiny claws to ascend up my pant legs, shirt, and finally sit on my shoulder. I was covered with little scratches, but enjoyed their company because I was living alone at the time.

Sadly for the pair—seldom had Istanbul street cats found the living so easy—Graeme was called back to Toronto. With no heart to return his houseguests to a life on the streets, he found a good home for them: "With a Turkish woman who owned a large house, and took care of stray cats."

He regretted saying goodbye, if not to life in Istanbul, but to his two adopted cats. Not for the last time would a creature needing a "hand-up," find it in the compassionate soul of Graeme Smith.

xxx

Fast forward to 2013, and find Graeme back in Afghanistan. He's now living and working in Kabul, the beautiful and ancient capital, situated alongside the Kabul River, wedged between the Hindu Kush Mountains and a narrow valley. Kabul is a world apart from the chaos of Kandahar Air Base where Graeme lived intermittently between 2006 and 2009, while working for the Globe and Mail.

Now as Senior Analyst for Crisis Group International in Kabul, he's living a domestic life with partner May Jeong, also a journalist. From this vantage point, Graeme keeps tabs on one of the world's enduring trouble spots.

There's a third member of the household too. Lying "over-easy" on a plush pillow, set in a deep windowsill and catching the rays of the afternoon sun is a small ginger cat. "We call her Pancake because her coat is the colour of the pancakes that I cook in the mornings." Life wasn't always so sweet for little Pancake.

Graeme explains that, in another life, the cat had belonged to Belinda Bowling, a journalist living in Kabul. "Belinda called her pet 'Screwdriver,' after the orange cocktail," says Graeme.

He tells the tale of how Belinda had taken Screwdriver in.

Belinda found the cat near death, cold and injured, in a snow-filled sewage ditch. Belinda thought the poor thing had been run over by a bicycle. She took the cat home and nursed her back to health.

Graeme notes that little Screwdriver was even mentioned in an article about her owner in the Financial Times. When Belinda was transferred out of Kabul in 2010, she made arrangements for her cat to live with the person who was moving into her house. That worked for a while, until the cat's second caretaker also moved out of the country.

> So Screwdriver was virtually left to fend for herself over another bitter Afghan winter. When we moved into the same house a few months later, she was hanging around, looking hungry and forlorn, clearly wanting to come in.

xxx

Graeme's heart was immediately captured by the needy creature. His girlfriend, May was less than thrilled.

> May was initially hesitant to even allow her into the house, because she looked so filthy and feral. But we did and after some generous feedings, she returned to health. We warmed up to her, and her to us.

A man with refined sensibilities, when it comes to naming pets at least, Graeme couldn't abide the name Screwdriver. "Especially when it got shortened to 'Screw,'" he comments. "Not a nice name for a lovely cat —especially one who'd needed to use her considerable wits to stay alive." They renamed her Pancake.

xxx

Our story does not end in creature comfort. Despite Graeme and May's best attempts to keep Pancake inside and safe, the lure of the wild has been a powerful one in her feral soul.

> We learned to never underestimate the willpower of our darling cat. She tries her best to slip outside in the evenings. Despite her history of suffering violence, perhaps there's something in her blood that makes her want to roam free — and maybe inflict a bit of violence, herself.

Pancake's risk-taking inclinations led her to losing yet another one of her anointed nine lives when Graeme and May moved to a different neighbourhood, with a new street cat population.

"Soon after we moved, one of us opened the door and zip! She was gone. From past experience we knew it was useless to try to catch her." What they witnessed over the next few minutes horrified them. Pancake became embroiled in a street scuffle with a much larger and stronger cat-warrior. Clearly wounded, she disappeared.

Five days later Pancake limped home. A piece of her leg was missing, torn off, it would seem, in the bloody fight. With daily treatment and love, May and Graeme nursed their cat back to health. "She's getting to be an old cat, but she's quite beautiful; she's happy and healthy," says Graeme, with affection. Despite being a geriatric, Pancake needs to be watched like a hawk.

> So, every night, we try to lure her indoors and then quickly lock all of the doors before she can get outside again. This was difficult at first, but the routine is getting easier. Maybe she's starting to understand the benefits of being protected.

And for the second time, a creature in need has chosen Graeme Smith to be a protector. Some things in life are just meant to be.

James and Stewart

Allan Slaight and Emmanuelle Gattuso

For more than half a decade, Allan Slaight's name has been synonymous with radio broadcasting in Canada. In 1948, Allan started as a radio broadcaster in Moose Jaw, Saskatchewan. By the early 1960s, he had moved up the broadcast ranks to become general manager of CHUM Radio in Toronto. In 1970, he purchased two radio stations in Toronto and Montreal. In 1985, Allan Slaight capped this meteoric rise by buying Standard Broadcasting Corporation Limited.

Meanwhile in Ottawa, Emmanuelle Gattuso was doing some climbing of her own. She had risen up the ranks of federal bureaucracy, becoming the communications director for the Commissioner of Official Languages. She went on to become senior VP public affairs at the Canadian Association of Broadcasters.

She and Allan met in Ottawa and married in July 1995. In a later interview, Emmanuelle noted that it was her future husband's "benevolence" that attracted her to him. He also shared some of the virtuous characteristics of her admired parents: the entrepreneurial spirit of her father and the humanitarian heart of her mother.

In 2007 Slaight sold his radio stations, 53 in total, as well as his two television stations, to Astral Media Inc.

Philanthropy has marked the lives of Allan and Emmanuelle. After Emmanuelle was diagnosed with breast cancer in 2002 and successfully treated at Toronto's Princess Margaret Cancer Centre, the couple made their gratitude known. In 2009 they initially donated

$12.5 million to create the Gattuso Rapid Diagnostic Centre at Princess Margaret. During the ensuing years, they donated a further $6.5 million, for a total of $19 million. This centre provides women diagnosed with breast disease with assessment, diagnosis and a treatment plan in one day. Then in early 2013, in what is the largest single donation for cancer research in Canadian history, the couple donated another $50 million to the Princess Margaret Cancer Foundation. The hospital called the donation "a game-changer in the future of cancer research."

Allan and Emmanuelle live in Toronto with their two beloved poodles, James and Stewart.

xxx

After her retirement, Emmanuelle desperately wanted a dog. But she knew she had her work cut out for her in convincing her husband, Allan, to go along with the plan. Emmanuelle says:

> We travelled a lot and he thought that a dog would just be a complication. But oh! I wanted one desperately. A poodle. I knew they wouldn't shed and were very intelligent—easily trained. And it had to be a female because I'd been told they were easier.

One day she saw an ad in a local newspaper for Chihuahua–Poodle mixes and against her better judgment, decided to go and see the pups. "I had no intention of getting a Chihuahua, so I have absolutely no idea why I set off in the first place," she laughs. She brought a friend along for a second opinion.

If the appearance of the home—rundown and unkempt—didn't give her second thoughts about the wisdom of her mission, the person who opened the door did. "My gosh. I thought I was seeing a real live witch." Nevertheless, the voyage of discovery continued. At one point the seller brought out a pail and dumped the contents in front of the two guests. Four tiny Chihuahuas and a black Poodle puppy tumbled onto the floor.

> And this little ball of fluff came right over to me. I knew it was a sign. Such a sweet, adorable black face, with a white chin, big brown eyes...but he was a male. No difference. At this point, I was a goner.

The pup was too young to take right now, but that would give her time to think up a name—a name her reluctant spouse could relate to. She had an epiphany.

> Since Allan was 16, he had been a great fan of magician Stewart James. He had read everything he could about this man. James wasn't your usual magician because he'd only done magic on the side of his real job as a postman in Courtright, Ontario. But he was very, very good and invented over one thousand magic tricks—with ropes and cards his specialty.

When Allan was older, he met his hero and the two became great friends. Stewart gave Allan his carefully written notes on his magic tricks and Allan decided to write a book on his hero. The result was "The Essential Stewart James".

When Emmanuelle knew she'd have some 'splainin' to do about a new dog, she was sure she'd have an easier time of it if the dog's name was James. And so, James the Poodle came to live with Emmanuelle and Allan—and became the love of Allan Slaight's life. Emmanuelle laughs heartily: "It was just a few months after we got James that Allan said to me: 'I just don't know how anybody can live without a dog!'"

Allan, a lover of "tricks" himself, taught James the standard doggie moves and then some. "And within five minutes James learned what Allan taught him," reports Emmanuelle.

xxx

Like many retired snowbirds, Allan and Emmanuelle escape to the south for at least part of the winter and keep a home in Florida. Of course, James would now come too. Being a small breed, the pooch could fly in his carrying crate in the cabin. But a bad experience one time caused the couple to rethink their travelling plans.

Emmanuelle was flying, business class, by herself, with James. Coming back home, she was stopped by airplane personnel who informed her that the dog would have to go in the cargo hold. The cage was too big to ride in the plane.

> I was upset and furious. I couldn't help it. No matter that all had been fine on the way over; this attendant said he had to go in baggage. And so my dear pet was sent to the cold, noisy and bumpy cargo hold.

She called Allan still in Toronto in tears and told him what had transpired. When the plane landed in Toronto, she anxiously awaited her "boy's" arrival.

> He was a wreck—shivering, frightened and whimpering. It took days to get him settled. The experience changed him when it came to travel of any kind. He didn't like to travel anywhere, even in a car.

To make sure this never happened again, Allan and Emmanuelle decided that from now on when they travelled a long distance with the dog, they would charter a private flight. They called it "James Air."

XXX

Two years after James came into the couple's life, Emmanuelle was in New York. She had the urge to check out one of the upscale dog accessory stores on Madison Avenue. But leashes and doggie sweaters left her brain when she came face to face with "the cutest little red poodle puppy I had ever seen." It was love at first sight.

Still she wondered how Allan would react to a second dog. She left the store dog-less—for a few minutes.

> I'd convinced myself that Allan would love this one too; that the little fellow would be company for James...and that we'd name him Stewart. So the tribute to Allan's hero, Stewart James, would be complete.

Emmanuelle hurried back to the store and bought the puppy. Within the blink of an eye, another customer who'd also been eyeing the red ball of fluff arrived and asked for the dog. "It was just meant to be," says Emmanuelle. "If I'd arrived a minute later she would have bought him."

Predictably, Stewart joined James in the Slaight–Gattuso Toronto household. And as it should be, Stewart became Emmanuelle's dog, to Allan's James.

James, now 11, and Stewart, 9, still bring their humans enormous love and affection. James' usual nighttime perch is the back of the living room sofa, but when Allan was feeling poorly after dental surgery, the pooch intuitively changed his routine to sleep on the bed at Allan's feet.

"How could anyone live without a dog?" say Allan Slaight and Emmanuelle Gattuso. How could they indeed?

Author's Note: Emmanuelle and Allan's beloved James passed away on November 28, 2013. He will always be in their hearts.

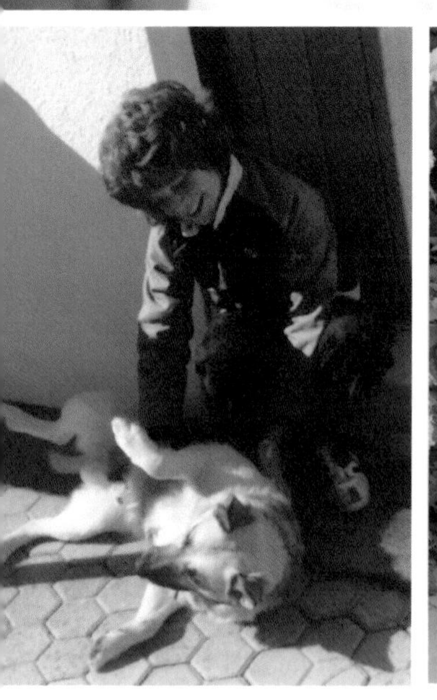

Jasper, Pongo and Ryder

Mark Cohon

Mark Cohon was born in Chicago but moved to Toronto in 1968 when he was two. His father, George, brought the family to Canada when George became the Founder of McDonald's Canada.

After high school, Mark returned to Chicago to attend Northwestern University. He then held a position as the head of corporate and game development with Major League Baseball International. This was followed by serving as the National Basketball Association (NBA) head of international marketing. He then moved on to President and CEO of Audience View ticketing.

In 2007, Mark Cohon became commissioner of the Canadian Football League. Longtime sports broadcaster Brian Williams calls him "the best thing that ever happened to the CFL."

Fascinated by science, and especially by wildlife, Mark's also been chair of the board of trustees of the Ontario Science Centre and has sat on the board of directors of World Wildlife Fund Canada.

Mark and his wife, Suzanne, live in Toronto with their daughter, Parker. They count as family members a 12-year-old Golden Retriever named Pongo and Ryder, a German Shepherd pup.

XXX

Mark Cohon's love of dogs had its start around his 13th birthday. He tells the story:

> I'd received some money as gifts for my Bar Mitzvah. A close friend of our family, Fred Turner (McDonald's Global CEO), asked me what my plans were for the cash. He suggested that I invest some of it, and gave me a tip for a gold stock that he thought would do very well for me.

Fred's heart was in the right place; his tip was not. Within six months, Mark's money had disappeared as the stock sank into oblivion. Fred felt terrible for steering the lad the wrong way and looked for a way to make it up to him. "I came home from school one day and found a beautiful Golden Retriever puppy," says Mark. "A present from Fred."

Once again Fred's kindness outshone his research. Jasper, the name that Mark chose for his golden-haired buddy, had been born in a puppy mill. By the time the pup was six months old, he had had several seizures. The Cohons rushed him to the Ontario Veterinary College in Guelph where he was treated. "My family has always been grateful to Guelph, who saved Jasper," states Mark. "The dog went on to live a long and happy life."

Dog ownership had only whetted young Mark's interest in the animal world. In high school, he scored a plum of a summer job as a zookeeper with the Toronto Zoo. He worked first in the North American domain, feeding and caring for polar bears and black bears. Later he moved to the Australasia domain with its elephants, tigers and various primates.

> I loved the job and had lots of opportunities to learn and grow. I fed the animals, shovelled their cages, and helped care for them when they were sick. I even had the opportunity of doing snake shows and giving lectures to kids.

His interest in wildlife continued during his university years. Home in Toronto after his third year of university, he had the chance to meet Joe MacInnis, world-renowned Canadian scientist, explorer and author. MacInnis had made the first scientific dives under the North Pole, and was an advisor to the Titanic discovery team that filmed the remains of the sunken liner in IMAX format.

MacInnis was also chair of Operation Raleigh Canada, an organization that sends students on science and service expeditions around the world. Mark's older brother had gone to Chile with the organization, but it was wrapping up its operations in Canada in 1988. Mark approached Joe with a new idea that would lead students on a polar expedition to Siberia and the Canadian High Arctic. Joe liked the idea. Mark's enthusiasm opened the door to another wildlife adventure.

In 1990, Mark served as expedition leader of Arctic Quest. It saw 30 Canadian and Russian students on a 12-week trek across the Arctic. Part of the group's time involved doing wildlife surveys on Baffin Island. This experience led Mark to seek more opportunities for wildlife adventure. When he was in his mid-thirties, he took a short break from work and set off for the island of Sumatra in Indonesia. He worked for a month with scientists seeking to reintroduce to the wild, orangutans that had been captured for zoos and through illegal trade. There, Mark picked up some vocabulary that would serve him well in the coming years. One phrase was Pongo abelii, the scientific name for Sumatran orangutan.

xxx

In 2001, following the Sumatran adventure, Mark found himself working in New York City. It also found him wanting a dog—a Golden Retriever, to be specific. And so Pongo, a three-month-old Golden began sharing Mark Cohon's life. He explains the seeming paradox of being a single working man and raising a pup in one of the world's largest cities.

> New York is actually a very friendly place for dog owners. You take your dog for walks and play at dog parks and you meet lots of friendly people. Dogs are an immediate door opener to socializing.

One evening, Mark found himself alone, sitting at a table on the patio of a busy New York bar. The lovely Pongo was at his feet. Across the room Mark caught the eye of a beautiful young woman.

At that moment, the crowd serendipitously thinned, creating a direct line of sight between the two strangers—one with an adorable puppy at his feet. "She saw Pongo and immediately came over to pet him," recalls Mark.

She was Suzanne Lucido, a New Yorker and dog lover. After chatting, the two exchanged email addresses. A day or so later, Suzanne received an email from Pongo. "He was asking her if she'd like to take him for a walk," Mark says, with a broad smile. Six months later, Suzanne and Mark were engaged. They married ten months after that.

xxx

With plans to move back to Toronto, Mark had time for one more New York experience. He met primatologist Jane Goodall, a woman he had admired since his youth. Kindred spirits, they soon became friends. Jane introduced Mark to Robert Schad, a wealthy industrialist who was involved with an organization called Earth Rangers.

Mark explains the group's mandate as "non-profit, working with young people in environmental education through interaction with wildlife—it challenged kids to get involved with their world." Jane urged Mark to become involved in helping Earth Rangers in Canada. She had no trouble convincing him.

On his return to Toronto, in addition to helping Earth Rangers, Mark became a member of the board of directors of the Ontario Science

Centre and later served as chair for seven years. His passion for wildlife also led him to join the board of directors of World Wildlife Fund Canada.

XXX

Now fully settled into Toronto life, Mark, Suzanne and daughter Parker Cohon are confirmed pet lovers. Pongo remains a healthy and active senior citizen at 12. He now shares the Cohon home with Ryder, a European-bred German Shepherd pup. The breed is a favourite of Suzanne's. Mark notes that the European-bred Shepherds have fewer health and gait problems, with a more "balanced" temperament than North American–bred German Shepherds.

The two Cohon dogs, while different in personality and temperament, are compatible. "Ryder's not the laid-back guy that Pongo is," admits Mark, "but still Pongo will put him in his place when he needs to." Ryder, bred to work and guard, is already protective of Parker, age seven.

Although for the present it seems that "the wild" has taken a back seat in Mark Cohon's life, he jokes: "Some might say that working in professional football, I've never left the animal kingdom!"

Jeremy Brett, Murdoch, Varley and Willie

Maureen Jennings

Born in Birmingham, England, Maureen Jennings emigrated to Windsor, Ontario, when she was a teenager. After receiving her degree in Psychology and Philosophy from the University of Windsor, and an MA degree in English Literature from the University of Toronto, she taught at Ryerson Polytechnic Institute in Toronto.

She later worked as a psychotherapist before devoting herself full-time to her writing. In 1997 her first "Murdoch Mysteries" novel, Except the Dying, was published. Six more "Murdoch Mysteries" novels followed.

In 2003, three of the novels were optioned to Shaftsbury Productions and CITY-TV to be produced as a television Movie of the Week. In 2007, Shaftsbury and CITY began production of "Murdoch Mysteries" as a television series.

Murdoch is not the only television adaptation of Maureen Jennings' books. Her story concept of a group of women working in a Canadian munitions factory during World War II has been developed into the CBC television series "Bomb Girls".

Maureen has also published two novels of a three-part World War II trilogy she's called "The Season of Darkness".

She is married to photographer Iden Ford and is the devoted parent of two dogs, Varley and Murdoch. She keeps the memory of her dear, departed Jeremy Brett close to her heart.

xxx

Maureen Jennings' sampling of pet ownership has been as eclectic as her life story. Some years ago, Watson, a beagle, whose sense of smell far outweighed his intellectual capacities, was joined in the Ford–Jennings home by as many as six Abyssinian cats. A lanky Siamese cat called Willie followed.

But it is Jeremy Brett, her brainy "I need to be busy" Border Collie, who holds the deepest and most enduring place in Maureen's heart. He was named after the British actor Jeremy Brett, who played Sherlock Holmes in the British television series.

The name surely suited Maureen's bundle of energy; like Brett's Holmes, Jeremy needed to be occupied and challenged. The dog-sport of agility was the means to this end.

xxx

Agility is a high-energy, fast-paced sport where a handler, working with a dog, manoeuvres through an obstacle course. Speed and accuracy determine the winner. Handlers are forbidden to come in contact with the dog during the course, and can only direct their charges using voice, movement and body signals.

No easy task is this. Competitive agility courses are complicated ones that involve multi-directional jumping over obstacles, weaving through tightly spaced poles, climbing ramps, balancing on see-saws and scooting through tunnels.

And while a fast, intelligent and obedient dog is integral to agility success, it's the handler who makes or breaks agility victory.

Border Collies, widely touted by experts to be among the most intelligent of breeds, excel at agility. When they're paired with a top-notch handler, they are virtually unstoppable on the course.

XXX

And so, Border Collie Jeremy Brett, bred for speed and intelligence, and his handler Maureen Jennings, no slouch in the brains department either, were a formidable team. Maureen frankly calls herself and her dog "obsessed with agility."

"The minute Jeremy heard his name announced at a meet, he was on—raring to go," recalls Maureen. "And he was absolutely brilliant at it. Jeremy just loved to compete."

Like a body-builder flexing his muscles before a match, Jeremy Brett would flash his teeth as he prepared to do his "stuff." "He was reactive and would get so wired that he'd start barking and barking and nothing could calm him down." Jeremy's focus was formidable too.

> Nothing could distract him from the task at hand. A herd of sheep could have trotted by and Jeremy would have ignored them. That's how focused and driven he was. That's what made him so good.

So good to be virtually unstoppable. The team of Brett and Jennings brought home numerous ribbons, trophies and medals from agility competitions. And when the team wasn't competing, they were practising. Maureen and Iden constructed practice equipment and laid it out in their backyard. A sure cure for Jeremy's "indoors antsies" was to head out for some agility practice.

They'd head for the park for soccer fun too. "He would move the ball and pass it, but was best in goal where he was unbeatable." Maureen jokes: "The only thing he couldn't do was play the violin, but I did teach him a trick on the piano."

Even given their successes, Maureen believes they could have been better.

> Jeremy was a brilliant agility dog. I was not a brilliant handler. To be one of these, you have to be able to plot and memorize the course ahead of time. You also have to be tack-sharp with your reactions. I had some problems with both of these.

After five years in competitive agility, Jeremy Brett began to slow down. His hips had begun to bother him. By now in her mid-sixties, Maureen too was feeling her years. "But it was important to keep Jeremy occupied—physically and mentally. Bored Border Collies become neurotic and destructive."

Maureen enrolled her dog in Rally-O, a less intense dog sport that combines agility with obedience. It didn't go over well with Jeremy. "He'd look at me like: 'What? This is for kids.'"

xxx

Maureen Jennings' love of dogs bubbles over in her novels. "I'll bring dog references in whenever I can," she laugh. In her first book of the series, "Except the Dying: A Murdoch Mystery", (Toronto: McClelland & Stewart, 1997) she introduces a shady character, Samuel Quinn, who is a dognapper.

Maureen's research into the era (Murdoch Mysteries is set in Toronto in the late 19th century) revealed that dognappers would employ a female dog in heat to lure "randy" purebred males into captivity. The dogs were kept until a reward was posted; then the lost dog would be returned with a nice bit of change for the napper.

Her conscientious care for animals plays out in her characterization of her main character, Detective William Murdoch. "It would be nice for Murdoch to have a dog but it's not realistic. He's never home to feed or walk a dog. My conscience won't let me write it."

In the fourth book of the series, "Let Loose the Dogs: A Murdoch Mystery" (Toronto: McClelland & Stewart, 2004), Maureen explored the dubious "sport" of ratting, popular around the turn of the 19th to 20th century. Rats were let loose, and then trained ratting dogs were set upon them. The dog that killed the most rats took home the money prize for his owner.

Maureen's action takes place with Detective Murdoch's ne'er-do-well father Harry pitting his dog Havoc against other ratters.

> "Flash the one to beat with forty kills," Lacey, the ring-keeper, called out. He released a cage of rats into the pit. They were dull brownish grey and fat from their summer feeding. At first they stayed close together, noses twitching, dazzled by the light. Lacey stirred them up with his crooked stick, then he shouted again.

"NOW! LET LOOSE YOUR DOG."

> Harry dropped Havoc into the ring. Immediately the terrier pounced on three rats in succession, killing each one with a single bite and a violent shake that broke their necks. The rest started to run, circling the small walled pit. Some tried in vain to climb up the smooth sides. For the next, long ten minutes the dog pursued them, biting, shaking, and dropping one after the other. The men took up the count, calling out the number of hits.
>
> "TWENTY-TWO...TWENTY-THREE...TWENTY-FOUR..."

The scene was a challenge to film. Maureen explains:

> Well, first of all, it's a lot more expensive to hire trained rats than trained dogs because there aren't as many of them. Then the trained rats we got were sleepy and didn't want to move around at first. So we had to stir them up a bit.

The interaction between dogs and rats was tricky too.

> To make sure the rats weren't harmed when we "let loose the dogs," all the filming had to be done with separate shots. The dogs and the rats were never together. The scenes were just

spliced together to make it appear they were fighting.

XXX

Maureen Jennings' dearly beloved Jeremy Brett passed away in September 2012. She had enjoyed his energy and intelligence, and even though she wanted to bring another dog into the household as companion for Varley, her rescue mixed-breed, she knew that her days parenting a Border Collie were past.

"The breed is so high maintenance and to be fair to them, they need an owner who is younger than a person in her seventies," she admits.

In the spring of 2013, Murdoch, a black Labradoodle joined the Jennings–Ford household. "I just couldn't resist the chance to say 'Murdoch, your office,'" she laughs.

LOVE!

Koko

The Right Honourable Kim Campbell

Born in Port Alberni, B.C., Avril (Kim) Campbell took leadership roles throughout her youth. At age 16, she became the first female student body president of her Vancouver high school. Since that time, she has spent much of her life breaking down barriers for women.

After law school, she entered public life, and held office in all three levels of government—municipal, provincial and federal. After her election to the House of Commons, she held several Cabinet positions: Minister of State for Indian Affairs and Northern Development; Minister of Justice and Attorney General; Minister of National Defence; and Minister of Veterans' Affairs.

She was the first Canadian woman to hold the Justice and Defence portfolios, and she became the first female Defence Minister in a NATO country. In 1993, she became leader of the Progressive Conservative Party and acceded to the position of Canada's 19th Prime Minister after Brian Mulroney's retirement. The next general election swept the Liberals back into power and she retired from politics.

Ms. Campbell was then named to two fellowships at the Harvard Kennedy School of Government. After serving as the Canadian Consul General in Los Angeles, she returned to the Kennedy School to teach in the Center for Public Leadership. She has since held advisory and senior positions on various high-level international governance and leadership boards.

Leadership for women in politics remains one of her key causes. One of the positions near and dear to her heart is on the Council of Women World Leaders. This organization is comprised of female heads of state and government. Kim Campbell has served as their chair. She is a founding member of the Club of Madrid, an organization of former heads of government and state who work to promote democratic values.

Today she continues her involvement in global issues, speaking widely on leadership, international politics, democratization, climate change, gender and Canadian/American relations.

Former Canadian Prime Minister Kim Campbell has had several beloved dogs over the years. She shares a fond memory from her childhood of one of them.

xxx

The little dog in the photo with me is Koko, our Japanese Spaniel. Koko was my first dog and came to us when I was around three years of age.

The circumstances behind Koko becoming our pet are somewhat cloudy. But I do know that my uncle had a girlfriend whose family bred these dogs. And they gave Koko to us as a gift. I am not sure why they were so generous. Alas! My handsome uncle did not marry their daughter, but Koko lived with us for many years.

Today Japanese Spaniels are not a common breed of dogs. They're also known as the Japanese Chin. They look similar to the Cavalier King Charles Spaniel or the Pekingese—but without the pushed-in face of the Peke. They weren't bred for any particular function like some breeds. Their history goes back to ancient Japan where they were the companions of the Japanese aristocracy. Queen Victoria, who was a great dog lover, had two Japanese Spaniels.

They are little dogs—only about twenty to twenty-three centimetres high and they weigh from four to six kilograms. Koko was fully grown in this photograph. Their coat colours are usually black and white, like Koko. But they can also be rust (called lemon) and white. The hair on their ears and tail is long and flowing.

Now about Koko's name: it came from Gilbert and Sullivan's Japanese operetta, The Mikado, in which "Koko" is one of the main characters.

xxx

We adored Koko, and aside from being great fun, he was very intelligent. The following episode demonstrates how clever and brave he was.

My family was living in Burnaby at the time, in an area that was still quite countrified—although it is now all built up. Past the house next door was an open field with horses. Behind our house, the next street was only partly built.

One night when my father was away, my mother—alone in the house with just my sister and me—heard footsteps coming up the back walk. She became very frightened because we were all in bed and she couldn't imagine who could possibly be coming to our house at that time of night. It was certainly no one we knew. Then something amazing happened.

Koko, hearing the unfamiliar steps, went into watchdog mode. He lowered his voice and started barking with a deep, ferocious sound. Then he began flinging himself against the back door. My mother was astonished. He sounded like a huge dog—more like a Rottweiler than a little lap dog! It was very clear that Koko was deliberately making himself sound large and fierce.

Whoever was coming to our house never made it to the door but simply disappeared. It must have been a stranger because our neighbours knew our dog was sweet and little and they wouldn't have been afraid.

I fondly recall as well Koko's best friend. She was a cat called Snowball. They were babies together and she taught him to bury his poop like a cat!

Koko was a wonderful dog. I have such sweet memories of him.

LOVE!

Leah and Wicket

Kurt Browning

Kurt Browning's name has been synonymous with Canadian figure skating for 25 years. In contrast to many of his peers who are newsmakers only during their competitive years, Kurt's light continues to shine brightly—both on and off the skating rink—long after his days of "6.0s" ended.

He first shot to national attention in 1989 when, as a talented lad from Caroline, Alberta, Kurt became the Canadian Men's Skating Champion. Over his glittering amateur career, he was a four-time Canadian Champion, a three-time Olympian, and a four-time World Champion. He was the first Canadian skater to win three consecutive World titles.

Innovation and exceptional athletic prowess were integral in the Browning achievements. In 1988, he became the first skater to successfully complete a quadruple toe-loop at a World's competition. He followed this feat by performing two triple Axels in the same original program, as well as a triple-Salchow/triple-loop combo. Neither had been successfully completed in competition before.

In 1994, Kurt retired from amateur competition. He continued to skate professionally, winning a number of professional skating competitions, including the Worlds, and since 1992 has been a member of the popular "Stars on Ice" troop.

Broadcasting has also called and Kurt was commentator at a number of Canadian and international skating championships. He worked for CBC at the Sochi Olympics and has also co-hosted the popular CBC program "Battle of the Blades."

He is married to Sonia Rodriguez, principal dancer with the National Ballet of Canada, and they have two sons. They share their Toronto home with Wicket, a rescue dog.

XXX

Growing up on a farm in central Alberta, Kurt Browning viewed dogs and cats more as farm helpers than house pets. Still, a feline named Kitty worked his way into young Kurt's heart.

> Kitty would follow my mom and me around the property, trailing behind us like a dog. But one day, he must have smelled a fox or some other predator because he raced up a tree and wouldn't come down.

Mom and son tried to coax the cat down, to no avail. They decided to leave him, thinking he'd find his way on his own. Still Kurt remained worried and after a while went back to the tree. There was Kitty, still clinging pitifully to a branch.

> I couldn't stand it so I climbed the tree higher than I was comfortable doing. The branch was wobbly and I was hanging on for dear life. Just as I within grabbing range, Kitty looked at me and I swear he grinned. Then, slick as anything, he scampered down the tree, leaving me to get down as best I could.

Cats!

XXX

Dogs moved into Kurt's life after he married Sonia. They needed a "hypo-allergenic" dog because of Sonia's mother's allergies and settled on a Portuguese Water Dog. Leah was her name.

A "Water Dog" would fit into their cottage-jump-in-the-lake lifestyle too. Ha! "Leah just didn't like water much," laughs Kurt. Except to rescue her family, it seems. "When I'd get ready to jump off the dock into the lake, she'd try to stop me by grabbing my swimming trunks. She'd occasionally grab a bit more than cloth too!"

When Gabriel, the couple's oldest son, went for a dip, Leah would take the plunge in hopes of "saving" her boy. The dog would swim in circles until Gabriel grabbed onto her tail and she towed him to land. "And with Sonia, whom Leah adored more than the rest of us, it was full rescue every time," laughs Kurt. "The only time she could get more than her feet wet was if we held Leah back."

In 2008, an invitation came Kurt's way that caused the Browning/ Rodriguez family to re-think their canine companion of choice. Kurt had been approached by the Pedigree dog food company to become their spokesperson. Pedigree was a supporter of shelter dogs and was launching a media campaign to persuade Canadians to consider adopting from a shelter instead of purchasing a dog from a breeder.

Kurt was a natural for the role. He travelled to various Canadian shelters doing interviews with shelter staff while camera crew featured some of the dogs looking for new homes. Along the way, he gained insight into the benefits of the work he was doing. This came after he and the crew visited a shelter in Peterborough, Ontario.

> They had a great, friendly Pit Bull who'd been waiting for its "forever home" for more than three years. The dog was so sweet that the shelter had adopted him as a mascot. They didn't want him to be euthanized but no one would take a chance on a Pit Bull.

The day after the Pedigree promo, which featured the needy guy, someone came forward. The next day the dog left with a loving new owner.

xxx

But Kurt soon realized he had a problem with his Pedigree role.

> I wasn't being a very honest spokesperson for shelter dogs, as we had a purebred dog that we'd gotten from a breeder. I realized that I was just the type of person the promos needed

to convince. And so I began to use that within the campaign.

When Leah passed away from cancer, the family practised what they preached. They did an online search of Ontario shelters for a dog that would fit their lifestyle. "And we found just what we were looking for in Wicket," says Kurt. He describes the family pooch, a mixed breed, as "looking like an Ewok from Star Wars." There were some early acclimatizing issues for both Wicket and the family, says Kurt.

> Wicket was nipping the boys but then I realized that it wasn't the dog's fault. The boys were provoking him. It wasn't his behaviour that needed to change, it was theirs. So we had to work on this.

And so with a bit of human behaviour modification, Wicket the shelter dog fit into the busy Browning/Rodriguez lifestyle. Not that there still isn't some horseplay. "The boys get him wound up so he'll chase them around the house. Not really safe but a whole lot of fun," admits Kurt.

Fun just seems to suit Kurt Browning's personality.

LOVE!

Lola, Romeo and Rosie

Marc Garneau

As a boy growing up in Quebec in the 1950's and 60's, Marc Garneau could scarcely have imagined that one day he'd fly in space. Still, there were youthful markers pointing him in that direction.

After graduating in 1970 from the Royal Military College in Kingston with an Engineering degree, Marc received a PhD in Electrical Engineering, in London, England. Further training in Halifax prepared him for his job with the Canadian Navy as a combat systems engineer.

In 1983, his life took an unexpected turn. He was selected out of four thousand applicants to begin astronaut training with NASA at the Johnson Space Center in Houston, Texas. The next year Marc Garneau became the first Canadian to fly in space as part of a NASA shuttle mission. Subsequently, he flew two more missions in 1996 and 2000. On his return to Canada from Texas in 2001, he served as president of the Canadian Space Agency.

Turning his sights to politics, Marc was elected in 2008 to the House of Commons for the Montreal riding of Westmount–Ville-Marie. He continues to represent that riding.

Marc, his wife, Pamela Soame, and their two children, Adrien and George, live in Montreal with two dogs.

XXX

A goldfish didn't count much as a pet, but it was better than nothing for young Marc Garneau. "My dad was a military man so our family moved around a lot. My parents felt that a pet didn't fit into that kind of lifestyle."

Absence didn't make young Marc's heart grow fonder either. "I was actually a little bit afraid of dogs—especially big ones, probably because I knew so little about them," he admits.

Growing into a petless adult, it was a case of "what you've never had you don't miss." But the status quo changed with his marriage to pet lover Pamela Soame. Marc admits with fondness:

> I call my wife the Mother Teresa of the pet world. At various times, she has rescued stray birds and dogs and can't resist petting stray cats. She loves all animals, but dogs especially.

The Bouvier des Flandres breed was a Pamela-favourite, because her parents had one. And she dearly wanted one. She knew that despite the Bouvier's size—big—and appearance—black and hairy—they were gentle and great family dogs. So, cautiously, Marc agreed.

xxx

Originating in Belgium, the Bouvier des Flandres breed has had a long history as a working dog—in police, search and rescue and on farms. Highly intelligent, they're known to have an "alpha personality" and are protective of their human family.

Most are black, grey or brindle in colour, and at a distance can have a remarkable resemblance to a bear. Occasionally a "rogue" fawn or cream-coloured pup can appear in a litter of black brothers and sisters.

xxx

So it was a fawn Bouvier that came to live in the Houston, Texas, home of Marc Garneau and Pamela Soame one fine day in 1995. And a fine Texan name she had—Texas Arundel Alamo Rose. Rosie for short.

Marc shares a family secret regarding Rosie's arrival.

> Pamela tells me, although I have no memory of this, that when I agreed to get the dog I said to her: "Well, it's okay, but you'll have to do the work." Then within a couple of days I was complaining that she was "hogging" the leash and I wanted my turn!

Rosie fit beautifully into the family, which eventually included sons Adrien and George. "The boys would climb all over her, grab her chew toys, put their hands into her mouth and she would never growl or complain."

Marc describes his dog's personality as calm and unperturbed. Still, Rosie showed her breed's patented protectiveness of family when strangers were close. At one hundred pounds, she was taken seriously.

As Rosie grew, so did her thick coat. One cool December evening, late at night, Marc and Pamela were out walking Rosie on a Houston golf course. They'd let her off leash as they had done, uneventfully, many times.

But this time she'd caught the scent of something and dashed off to investigate. By the time Rosie returned it was clear what had attracted her attention. "It was a skunk and she had been well sprayed on her hindquarters," says Marc. With a "mane" the thickness of Rosie's, this was no small matter.

> It was too late to call a groomer or the vet and it was too cold to leave her outside. So we put her in the laundry room for the night and stuffed towels under the door to try to prevent the horrible smell from infiltrating the rest of the house. It didn't work very well.

Bright and early the next morning, Rosie was whisked to a groomer for some much-needed attention. Still, it was a couple of weeks before all the skunk odour left Rosie's curly locks.

Bred originally as farm working dogs, Bouviers instinctively like to herd. Rosie's family got an idea how much this genetic trait still lingered one day when they, Rosie included, went to visit friends at a Texas ranch.

> She spotted the Brahma cattle—rather fearsome big guys with horns—and immediately tried to round them up. They weren't the least bit intimidated. They just looked at her as if to say—"What are you doing? Relax, we're not going anywhere."

XXX

In 2001, with Marc's astronaut career at an end, the Garneau family returned to Canada. The cooler Canadian climate was perfect for Rosie, now well past five. "She particularly loved the snow and she would plunge into it and bury her head, looking for something she had smelled below the surface," Marc remembers.

Then one day Rosie wasn't herself. She was lethargic and her appetite was off. A trip to the vet produced bad news. Like many large breed dogs, Bouviers, even those in the prime of life like Rosie, are prone to cancer. Tests showed that she had a cancerous colon tumour. Marc remembers this difficult time:

> We had to decide what to do. Chemotherapy was an option although an expensive one. In the end, we elected to do everything we could for her. She started on medication and underwent a series of chemotherapy treatments.

At the recommendation of the Garneau's veterinarian, who had researched the different possible options, Pamela went to the Oncology Pharmacy of the Royal Victoria Hospital to buy the human chemotherapy drugs that would be administered to her beloved pet. Marc recalls the reaction Pamela received.

> It wasn't easy explaining to the person behind the counter

> that Rosie did not have a medical card. When the pharmacist told Pam to make sure the patient was informed of the possible side effects of the drugs, she explained that the patient was our dog Rosie.

Surprised, the pharmacist still wished Pamela well and informed her that many of the approved drugs used today are initially tested on animals. Rosie responded well to the treatment and her health improved over the next 18 months. The cancer was in remission and the Garneau family was overjoyed.

Then as all too often happens, Rosie's cancer returned, with a vengeance. This time there was little that could be done. When Rosie's time came, Marc and Pamela asked their veterinarian to euthanize their dearly beloved Rosie at home.

> Our vet, who deeply loves his work, had us all gathered around Rosie in her favourite corner of the living room. He explained everything to our boys, three and six at the time. And then she gently drifted off to "sleep."

After Rosie died, the veterinarian gently lifted one of her big furry feet and held it up to his nose. "We thought this was perhaps related to the diagnosis and asked him." The veterinarian's answer surprised them. "He said he loved the smell of old dog feet. We were touched by this and it helped us get through the moment," recalls Marc.

While Rosie's death deeply affected both Pamela and Marc, it was the more recently converted dog lover who felt the pain intensely.

> Maybe it was because I had never had pets as a kid and had never gone through the experience of losing them like Pamela had. It was a very sad and difficult time for me.

The extent of Marc's grief surprised him. "I'd heard people talk about how the loss of a pet had affected them but I had no idea how that felt. Now I did."

Rosie was cremated. When Marc next returned to Houston, he wanted to bring her ashes in order to scatter them in the park where the family had so often walked their beloved girl. A few roadblocks stood in the way. Passing through airport security, he was asked to open his carry-on bag, which contained Rosie's ashes in a plastic container. It was labelled "Rosie's ashes."

> I explained that I wanted to bring the ashes back to Texas. The guard, who obviously assumed that Rosie was a human relative, was most respectful and offered his deep condolences.

Marc remembers releasing Rosie's ashes into the wind in "Rosie's Park":

> I felt a little self-conscious even though no one was around at the time. Most of all, I felt both sad and happy. Sad because scattering Rosie's ashes was a final act; happy because a flood of happy memories filled me as I threw handfuls of her bodily remains into the air.

xxx

Now a confirmed pet lover, Marc has since welcomed a Golden Doodle named Lola and a part-Lhasa Apso–part Maltese pup named Romeo to the house.

He looks at the relationship his two boys have with their dogs and compares it to his reticence as a child.

> My kids have benefited enormously from having pets—having the responsibility of taking care of them but also loving them and spending time with them. It's something I missed in my childhood and I am so glad I can give this to my own children.

LOVE!

Magnus and Seamus

Rick Hansen

Born in 1957 in Port Alberni, British Columbia, the youthful Rick Hansen loved two things in life: fishing and sports. He excelled at both. Then in 1973, at the age of 15, his life changed irrevocably. Coming home from a fishing trip with two teenage friends, the pick-up truck the boys were riding in crashed. Rick was thrown from the back of the vehicle, and sustained a serious spinal injury. He was paralyzed from the waist down.

With the support of family, friends, teachers and coaches, Rick picked up the pieces of his shattered life and vowed to move on. As before his injury, sports played an integral part of Rick's rehabilitation. Over the coming years, Rick Hansen won 19 international wheelchair marathons, as well as the world title four times. At the 1982 Pan American Wheelchair Games, he won 9 gold medals, and he represented Canada at the 1984 Olympics. Rick was named Canada's Disabled Athlete of the Year in 1979, 1980 and 1982.

In 1982, Rick enrolled at the University of British Columbia (UBC), later becoming the first person with a physical disability to graduate with a degree in Physical Education from UBC.

More goals were on his horizon. In March 1985, at the age of 27, Rick set off from Vancouver to wheel forty thousand kilometres through 34 countries on his Man In Motion World Tour. His goal was to prove the potential of people with disabilities. His gruelling tour took 26 months and raised $26 million.

After the tour, Rick established the Rick Hansen Foundation. Its mission remains to find a cure for paralysis after spinal cord injuries. The foundation also works to create more accessible and inclusive communities. The Rick Hansen Foundation has since raised $291 million.

Rick, his wife, Amanda, and their three daughters, Emma, Alana and Rebecca live in Richmond, British Columbia, with their beloved pets. They are Magnus, a 15-year -old Nova Scotia Duck Tolling Retriever, and Seamus, an orange tabby.

XXX

When Rick and Amanda Hansen decided that they wanted to bring a dog into their family of five, their youngest daughter, Rebecca, was only three years old. So they did their canine homework first.

> With our three girls still very young at the time, we wanted a dog that would fit well into our family—smart and easy to train. We also wanted our pet to be a great companion and gentle with kids.

And as seems only fitting for the family of a true Canadian hero, they decided on a 100 percent Canadian breed of dog. The Nova Scotia Duck Tolling Retriever was developed in that province.

Smaller than its "cousins," the Golden and the Labrador Retrievers, Tollers were developed in the 19th century. They toll (lure) curious ducks by making a disturbance at the edge of the water. Foxes are said to attract quarry in a similar way.

With a dense, water-repellent, reddish-golden coat, Tollers are characterized by tidy white feet and white markings on the chest. The white tip of the Toller's tail is a visual lure to the unsuspecting ducks. All that talent and a family dog too!

XXX

Having decided on the breed, the Hansen family visited a breeder to pick out their puppy. Rick describes how the selection was made.

> There were seven puppies and five of them were all bunched together running around and being puppies. There were two over to the side by themselves. One was the runt of the litter and the other seemed to be nurturing and protecting the runt from the others. We decided right away that this little loving caretaker was the dog for us.

And so in 1998, Magnus, the Nova Scotia Duck Tolling Retriever, came to live in the Hansen household. Fifteen years later, and now a senior citizen, Magnus continues to make an indelible mark on the family's hearts.

Rick laughs that only in one area has he fallen short of expectations. Magnus, the duck dog, doesn't like water. When he was a pup playing with his "people" by the Hansen backyard pool, Magnus fell into the deep water.

"We got him out right away, but the experience scared him," says Rick, "and he avoids deep water." Days at the beach from that point on saw Magnus barely getting his tidy white feet wet. Sometimes this takes some explaining to curious onlookers.

Years ago, Amanda decided to take Magnus to a Duck Tolling "picnic" being held on the banks of the Fraser River. When Amanda and Magnus returned home, Rick asked how things had gone. Amanda answered with a shake of her head:

> Anyone watching would have seen a whole army of Duck Tollers splashing and swimming and having the time of their lives in the river. Except one...and that was Magnus. He was as far away from the fun as he could be!

Magnus has strengths in other areas, says Rick. He loves bicycling. Rick powering his hand-driven bicycle and Magnus on a long leash running beside him are familiar sights in the Hansen neighbourhood. Often Rick's friend and neighbour, Ralph, and his Golden Retriever make it a foursome. Their route takes them through the woods so it's not unusual to have an errant squirrel or chipmunk dart by.

> And Magnus is off! More than once, if I'm not on my toes to brace myself and secure the leash, he's after a squirrel. So he goes one way and I go the other. I've done more than one face plant.

At 15, Magnus is slowing down...a bit. A few years ago, he was diagnosed with Addison's disease. A disorder of chronic adrenal insufficiency, Addison's strikes both humans and dogs. Both must rely on regular medication.

Rick believes that Magnus' little pills contain some elixir of youth. "I think I need to be taking some of those pills," Rick laughs.

> Because for fifteen, he's in great shape, with energy and his passion for life—and squirrels. Magnus is pretty territorial too. He's very protective of his home turf and of us, his family.

One day, by accident, an unsuspecting delivery boy found out just how protective Magnus was. Rick tells the story.

> My buddy and bike-riding partner Ralph and I play practical jokes on each other. One day he planned to drop over before we went bike-riding with the dogs.
>
> So I decided I was going to get Magnus revved up in his "I've gotta protect my people" role. When the doorbell rang and I opened the door, expecting to see Ralph, I let Magnus loose—just for fun to scare the be-jeepers out of my buddy.

What Rick didn't know was that one of his daughters had ordered pizza delivery. When the delivery boy rang the doorbell, he could hear the sound of a ferocious dog inside.

> As I opened the door, shouting "Get him, Magnus," I saw who it was. The poor pizza guy was scared out of his life by the charging dog who was being egged on by the guy inside!

Rick adds that he immediately contained Magnus, and apologized. Magnus then bestowed a doggie kiss on the delivery boy.

Aside from his interest in squirrels and other fast-moving forest creatures, Magnus is as gentle as a newborn lamb and totally devoted to his family—especially to Rebecca Hansen. "Magnus and Rebecca grew up together and they have a very special bond," says Rick. When Rebecca was growing up she'd never leave the house for school without scratching Magnus behind his ears so that she could carry his special scent all day.

xxx

For the past five years, Magnus has shared his people with Seamus, a handsome orange-coloured tabby. A social-butterfly-type of feline, Seamus has a regular route through the neighbourhood, stopping to visit at various houses. "He'll walk in, say hello, get a couple of pats and then is off," laughs Rick.

And when he chooses to come home, Seamus clearly is dominant over the "I just wanna please everybody" Magnus.

> Magnus loves Seamus and the two of them will play—when Seamus will give the poor dog the time of day. But to see the two of them, their coats the same colour, curled up together sleeping is just so sweet.

Occasionally, the Hansen pets have a higher purpose than play. Rick explains jokingly:

> I'll have been away travelling for a few days and I'm missing my family. So I can hardly wait to get home to see them. I come in the door, the girls say "Oh hi Dad, gotta go" and Amanda is busy or gone somewhere too.
>
> But Magnus is overjoyed to see me. "Oh Dad, I'm so happy you're home, can I kiss you?" and even Seamus will get on my lap and sing me a purr. Thank goodness for these guys!

Raised with pets as a child, Rick is an unabashed fan. "Pets, dogs especially, ask so little and give so much unconditional love. I cannot imagine living in a home without them."

Author's Note: Over the course of creating this book Magnus passed away. Thank you to Rick Hansen for sharing his story and kind words.

> Losing our beautiful dog Magnus was heartbreaking for the whole family. He was 16-years-old and lived a long and good life. He was a gift from God to our family and he brought much love and joy to us all. He will be missed very much indeed! – Rick Hansen

LOVE!

Midi, Shrodie and Sweet Pea

Jann Arden

Born and raised in Calgary, Jann Arden Richards had her first public singing gig at her high school graduation. Her sights had been set on becoming a teacher, but a performing life beckoned too.

At age 18, Jann recorded her first record in 1980, called Never Love a Sailor. It would be 13 years before she would record another. In the meantime, she began playing guitar and singing in bars around the Calgary area. She supplemented her meagre income with a variety of part-time jobs. One was as a ball-washer at a local golf course and another as a singing waitress.

It was a rough and uncertain life, but one day a "guardian angel" by the name of Neil McGonigle heard her sing and saw real potential. McGonigle, a music manager, challenged Jann to decide whether she was serious about her music. If she was, McGonigle suggested she give him a call.

She did. And it changed her life. Under McGonigle's shepherding, in 1993 Jann's first CD, Time for Mercy, was released. It was an acclaimed hit. A string of singles including "I Would Die for You" catapulted Jann to international prominence. That year she won the Canadian Juno Award for Best New Performer and Best Video. Since then, Jann has released 11 albums. Seventeen of her songs have been Top 10 hits. She's won eight Juno Awards.

But "singer-songwriter" is only part of the Jann Arden package. She's published two books, "If I Knew Do You Think I'd Tell You?" and "I'll Tell You One Damn Thing". Her third book, "Now Falling Backwards", was released in 2013. Jann also hosts a summer show on CBC Radio called "Being Jann".

She lives outside Calgary with her dog, Midi, and her cat, Sweet Pea.

xxx

Jann Arden keeps those she loves close. "I look out my window and there is my mom and dad's house sixty feet away from mine." She laughs that it was supposed to be a "granny cottage" but it grew. She's on the road a lot, but when she's home, the three of them visit daily. One of their favourite relaxation activities is watching movies in the movie theatre that Jann has built in her home.

Jann's pets fall into the "beloved" category too. When she was nine, the family moved out of Calgary to a country acreage. They set up household in a trailer for a couple of years until finances allowed more permanent housing. The cramped spacing didn't stop the family, animal lovers all, from gathering pets around them. Birds were a favourite, especially with Jann's mom, Joan.

> Mom is a real bird lover and she was always finding abandoned or injured birds and nursing them back to health. One was a magpie with a broken leg that she kept in a shoebox till it could get around. She also kept two geese called Easter and April who followed her around the property.

Rabbits, various dogs and cats came to stay too. The dogs were especially valued as they warned against the regular presence of coyotes in the neighbourhood. As a country kid, Jann also learned the reality of life and death for farm animals.

> I was at a neighbour's farm when the pigs were being slaughtered. I'll never forget the knife going across their throats and the red blood gushing out. I was horrified but the kids I was with had no reaction. You learned to be thick-skinned as a farm kid, I guess.

xxx

As an entertainer, for the past 20 years road trips have been a part of Jann's routine. Originally, she felt this precluded having a pet dog.

Cats were more flexible. And Jann did love cats. So Shrodie, from the Calgary SPCA, came into her life. Shrodie had a big personality and a big purr to go with it—so much so that Jann gave him credit for "purrcussion" on the song "When You Left Me" from her 2003 album "Love Is the Only Soldier".

Then one day Shrodie disappeared from Jann's yard.

> He was a savvy guy and knew the neighbourhood so I wasn't worried at first. But after a couple of days, I was beside myself. I went door to door asking if anyone had seen him. I put posters with his picture on telephone poles and in stores and offered a reward.

Jann had heard of a "pet detective" in Calgary who sleuthed out missing animals and she hired him—with no results. Her next step was a pet psychic.

> She told me that Shrodie was still alive. So that gave me hope and I kept calling the SPCA every other day. But when three months passed and Shrodie didn't return, I'd pretty well given up. I missed having a cat so much that I went to the SPCA and came home with two kittens.

Then one day she got a call from the SPCA. Turns out one of Jann's neighbours had discovered a duffle bag on her doorstep. And the bag was moving. Plucking up her courage, the neighbour opened the bag. Inside was a cat hissing and spitting and spray-painted red. A hand-written message was attached to the cat that said "Happy Christmas."

She immediately took the cat to the SPCA who, even under the red camouflage recognized it as Jann Arden's missing cat Shrodie. They called her. "I was in tears when I saw Shrodie. He recognized me and asked to be picked up."

The mystery of the cat-napped-spray-painted cat was never solved.

Jann took Shrodie to a groomer who shaved off most of the red Christmas decoration. Gradually, the rest grew out. The bigger challenge was getting Shrodie accustomed to the young kittens who'd moved in while he'd been away.

Despite his trauma, Shrodie lived to the ripe old age of 18. "Then one day he wandered off," recalls Jann. "I looked for him but never found him. I think he went somewhere to die. Cats are like that."

xxx

Jann Arden's home away from home is Nashville. "I have great friends in the music business there," she says. One of her friends had a lovely white Malti-Poo (Maltese–Poodle cross) named Midi after singer Bette Midler. But the friend's circumstances changed and she was going to have to find a new home for her dog. She asked Jann if she'd like to become Midi's new dog-parent. And to Jann Arden's great surprise she said yes. "The only dogs we'd had when I was growing up were big dogs. I knew nothing about life with a little dog and here I was with one. Go figure!"

But it became a match made in heaven. Small enough to fit in a carrying case, quiet and adaptable to new environments, Midi started travelling with Jann—on airplanes, trains, buses and cars. "I buy the seat beside me when we're travelling by air and she sits in her case for the flight."

Travelling from city to city on the tour bus is ideal because Midi is out of her cage and "holding court" with the band and other staff. As for train travel and VIA's hard and fast rule about pets riding in the baggage compartment, Jann holds her tongue!

xxx

Having a travelling companion—one who depends on her for care—has changed Jann's life on the road.

> Before Midi, I'd never leave the hotel once I got there until

> it was time to leave for the show. It was just easier if I ate in my room, maybe went down to the gym and watched TV. Pretty boring. But now I have to get out—to walk the dog. So I talk to people and they talk to me. It's much better than the way I lived before.

Jann's routine after the show has changed too. Even though she's left Midi to be cared for by a dog-sitter when she's onstage, she's anxious to get back to her pet.

> Before it was too easy to stay after the show, have some drinks with the band, get back to the hotel late and sleep late in the morning. But I can't and I won't do that anymore. I need to get back to Midi, get her out for a walk. It helps me unwind too.

xxx

Jann Arden's generosity for animals doesn't stop at her pets. After the disastrous Calgary flood in the summer of 2013 that did $50-million damage to the Calgary Zoo, she's lent her time and financial support to the animals. An Arden-penned song "Two-by-Two Rebuild the Zoo" has been the theme song for the rebuilding efforts. Jann performed it at the fund-raiser to kick off the campaign.

Big voice—that Jann Arden. Big heart too.

Milo

Lynda Boyd

Show business has run through Lynda Boyd's veins since she was a child growing up in Vancouver. A photo of her at age five shows her in a clown costume and makeup as part of a kids singing and dancing chorus line.

She earned her living first in music, touring Western provinces with her band "The Blenders". Live theatre followed, and for several seasons Lynda was a featured performer at Vancouver's Arts Club Theatre. Film acting then called, in both Canada and the U.S. A self-described "late bloomer," she moved to Los Angeles where acting jobs were more plentiful when she was 41.

In 2009, Lynda was chosen to play the role of Rose in the popular CBC series "Republic of Doyle", shot in St. John's, Newfoundland. One season she was nominated for a Gemini Award (Canada's Emmy) for her work.

Performing is only part of the multi-talented Lynda Boyd's profile. She's a great believer in giving back to her community too. St. John's fills that niche now and she's taught acting classes, adjudicated at a drama festival and has become a spokesperson for the "Warm Hearts Campaign" in aid of Iris Kirby House, a shelter for women and children.

Lynda shares her life with her beloved dog Milo.

XXX

Singer, actress and writer Lynda Boyd quickly affirms the notion that being in show business predicts a jet-setting life.

> When I was living in Los Angeles I got an acting job that had me flying to Winnipeg for one day of filming every week. It wasn't practical for me to move to Winnipeg but I couldn't afford to turn it down either. I had to work.

There was more in the travelling mix.

> That same summer, I was concurrently shooting a mini-series in Halifax and a feature in Vancouver. Every few days, I was at a different airport, in a different van, at a different hotel... but the flying was the hardest part. Ironically, I had always wanted a career that involved travel because it seemed so glamorous to me as a child growing up.

But the reality was far different than Lynda's childhood fantasies. In fact, flying made her anxious—very anxious. And, to make things even more stressful, it always seemed that when Lynda was in the air, there was turbulent weather. "Thunderstorms and lightning bolts frazzled me," she says.

The situation got so severe that she was eventually diagnosed with a clinical anxiety disorder. Knowing that flying would continue to be part of her life as long as she remained in show business, she looked for ways to alleviate her stress.

> I'd been thinking of getting a dog for companionship for some time anyway. But as my anxiety bouts got worse, I started to investigate getting a service dog to assist me. My therapist confirmed that this this could be a very good thing.

She started doing some online research, matching her personality and lifestyle with the best breed of dog. But one criterion was predominant. As the dog would be travelling with her, it would need to be a small breed—small enough to meet airline guidelines for dogs flying in the plane's cabin. Lynda had no intention of stowing her dog in the hold.

The perfect match was found on Kijiji, the online buy-and-sell site. Lynda found a litter of Malti–Poo–Chi's—a hybrid mixture of Maltese, Poodle and Chihuahua—in a fetching mix of black, grey and white.

"The pups were about four pounds when I saw them. The breeder said they would grow no more than about ten pounds," recalls Lynda. She knew immediately that she'd found her forever friend.

Naming him was more difficult.

> At first I thought he should have a human name. So he was Walter for a few days; but that didn't stick. Then I thought "Buddy." That was a friendly sort of name. But that just wasn't right either. Then I came up with Bear—because he looked like a little black bear from the back. But you know I just wasn't set on Bear either. This was so hard...

It was Lynda's veterinary assistant who came up with the perfect moniker. "He looks like a Milo...yes, yes he does indeed," she said. And he did! Milo's personality was perfect too. "He was calm, even as a puppy," says Lynda, as she pulls out her photos. They show a sweet rascal, but one somewhat larger than the predicted ten pounds. Lynda laughs:

> He now weighs twenty-five pounds so I'm still not certain what mix he is. Certainly not what the breeder said. I had his DNA tested and they came back with fifty percent Border Collie, and a bunch of other breeds like Dalmation and Saint Bernard.

XXX

The requisite puppy classes for Milo followed. At the same time, Lynda was also working on having her dog designated an Emotional Support Animal (ESA). She located a Service Dog organization which, with the requisite documentation from Lynda's therapist, would provide Milo with a working dog vest and tags. These would identify him as a certified ESA. The organization would also provide official documentation for Lynda to carry and present when she was flying.

Milo quickly learned his role. On an airplane, he sits quietly at Lynda's feet. Intuitively he gives her the gentle reassurance she needs in the air. Especially when there is turbulence, which causes Lynda's anxiety levels to soar, she pulls him close and buries her face in his fur. "Just his touch seems to calm me," she offers.

Not that travelling with a service dog is always a walk in the park. Lynda's found that having an "invisible disability" causes some roadblocks, especially passing through security checks.

> Despite the fact that Milo is wearing his service vest, I've had more than one airport employee tell me: "You've got to have that dog in a crate, lady." Because I'm not blind or in a wheelchair and they can't see my disability, they don't understand.

In these situations, Lynda adopts a non-confrontational attitude, pulling out her documentation and explaining: "Under the Human Rights Code, asking me to produce proof of my disability is not required." Nevertheless, not wanting to change the world, but just get herself and Milo where they need to go, Lynda doesn't press her point.

XXX

Life in St. John's has done much to dispel Lynda Boyd's anxieties too. Her regular "gig" on "Republic of Doyle" has given her a sense of security. The show is currently wrapping work on its fifth season, with high ratings.

She's bought one of St. John's delightful, brightly-painted homes near the base of historic Signal Hill. She and Milo keep in shape with at least one walk per week up the historic hill that overlooks St. John's Harbour.

> I love St. John's for many reasons. Size is high on the list. Especially when you compare it to Vancouver, St. John's is still a small town. You can get anywhere you need to be in the city in minutes, not hours. I like that a whole lot!

At home, Milo is "on guard" for his human. He responds to any knocks at the door or any irregularity outdoors by serious barking. "Even with the same mailman who comes pretty well the same time each day, he'll alert me," Lynda reports. She doesn't mind one bit. Lynda adds that Mike, the father of "Republic of Doyle" star Alan Hawco, has the job of delivering new scripts to the homes of the show's actors.

> Mike says he can judge whether I'm home or not even before he reaches the door and knocks. If I'm home, Milo barks. If I've stepped out for a time and have left him at home alone, he's quiet. Then Mike just leaves the script.

As time passes, the bond between Lynda and Milo deepens. "He's even taken on some of my characteristics—not all good ones," she jokes. "Like a nervous stomach and an anxious nature and um, the list goes on...." She calls her beloved dog "a mirror of me."

Dog-less for most of her peripatetic adult life, Lynda wonders how she got along before. "Milo has played such a large part helping me deal with some of the issues I struggle with," she acknowledges. "He is really a part of me."

Miso and Pu-Yi

Chantal Petitclerc

Ironically for Chantal Petitclerc athletics only played a significant part in her life after a serious injury left her a paraplegic. Born in Saint-Marc-des-Carrières, Quebec, Chantal was 13 when a barn door fell on her. The determined teenager took up swimming, which pushed her to stay active. It also allowed her to gain physical strength while confined to a wheelchair.

At 18, she took part in her first wheelchair race. She was immediately hooked on the sport and trained relentlessly for competitions. A short four years later, she competed in the 1992 Barcelona Paralympic Games, and won two bronze medals in wheelchair racing. Over the next four Olympics and Commonwealth Games, Chantal won 19 additional medals. The 2008 Beijing Summer Paralympics and Olympics was Chantal's biggest medal "haul." She returned to Canada with five gold medals and two new world records. For her achievements, Chantal Petitclerc was awarded the Lou Marsh Trophy as Canadian Athlete of 2008.

She remains the only Canadian to have won gold medals at the Olympics, Paralympics and Commonwealth Games. Her 21 gold medals are the most of any wheelchair athlete.

After retiring from competition, Chantal has remained active in the sports movement. She will act as Canada's Chef de Mission for the 2014 Glasgow Commonwealth Games.

Chantal and her husband, James Duhamel, share their Montreal home with two exotic cats.

XXX

Chantal Petitclerc says that she used to be a dog person. The 14-time Paralympic gold medal winner in wheelchair racing, and holder of 14 Olympic records, eventually came to realize that cats better suited her peripatetic lifestyle.

"Originally I didn't think that cats were as interesting as dogs," she laughs. That was before she met her beloved Pu-Yi, an exotic Singapura, and Miso, an Abyssinian. "I've come to see cats as much more fascinating creatures than dogs," she says. "They have a secret life that you don't know much about. Dogs wear everything on the outside."

Once the decision was made to be cat people, Chantal and her husband, composer James Duhamel, started researching various breeds. They were especially intrigued by the exotic Abyssinian, the so-called Border Collie of the cat world.

"Abbys" are intelligent, adventurous, assertive and interminably curious. With eyes of either gold or green and ticked coats in four colours—red, blue, fawn or ruddy, they're gorgeous creatures too. The Petitclerc–Duhamels found a breeder in Quebec City and went to visit.

What Chantal and James didn't know when they paid their call was that the breeder also raised Singapuras. The smallest of the cat breeds, with adult females as light as four pounds, Singapuras are distinguished by their "sepia agouti"-coloured coats, oversized ears and huge eyes.

With a personality in direct contrast to their petite build, these little dynamos seem to be always in the middle of anything their human family is doing. "Pests" is a favourite description of the endearing Singapura.

"We just couldn't make up our minds between the two breeds," laughs Chantal. "So we brought home one of each." They named their Abyssinian "Miso," but not after the soup, jokes Chantal. Their little Singapura would officially go by the Oriental-sounding "Pu-Yi," but informally is called "the big guy." Chantal explains the confusion:

> When we got them, Pu-Yi was older than Miso and the bigger of the two. So he was "the big one" and Miso "the little one." Even when Miso grew bigger than his brother, his "baby name" stuck and he has always been "the little one."

xxx

Chantal soon found that her two cats were welcome "good medicine" as she trained gruelling hours for the 2004 Olympics in Athens, and later the 2008 Olympics in Beiijing.

> I'd come home so tired and there would be the cats, playing and jumping around and being just so entertaining and relaxing. You had to laugh at them. As I watched them, I began to think that cats seem to have their own worlds. You really never know what's going on with them in their little cat minds.

While the two breeds were closely related, they showed quite different personalities. Miso, the Abby, was clearly the climber. Chantal and James have provided climbing apparatus for their height-loving boy. "He's the more dominant of the two, being bigger and stronger," states Chantal. "He'll push Pu-Yi out of the food bowl if he thinks he should be first."

Miso's attention is directed more to James and he likes to wind himself around his human's legs. "He's rubbing on his scent," says Chantal, "so I think it's a dominance thing." The petite Pu-Yi likes her "Mom" best and in true Singapura style loves to be a distraction when Chantal is trying to work on her computer.

Chantal and James have made the decision not to declaw their cats. They've provided scratching posts instead. Vet appointments happen at home. "It was just far too crazy and the cats were too stressed out the only times we took them out to the veterinarian."

xxx

After the 2008 Olympics, Chantal retired from competitive wheelchair racing. She has continued to keep in top shape participating in marathon wheelchair road marathons.

As the 2014 Glasgow Commonwealth Games, where she will act as Chef de Mission, creep ever closer and preparations accelerate, she's frequently away from home. She sorely misses her "boys" when she's away, but notes that even after she's been absent for some time, the cats seem not to take much notice when she returns.

> Not like dogs, who are so openly affectionate and go a little crazy when you come back. You always know what's on a dog's mind. But with cats, you just never know what they're thinking. Like a woman...I like that!

LOVE!

"The Three Totos": Neddy, Tilley and Winny

Terry Shevchenko

In 1899 in Chicago, L. Frank Baum, a former actor and newspaper editor who dabbled in writing children's literature, had a bright idea for a new book. It revolved around Dorothy Gale, a Kansas farm girl who is blown to a magical land named Oz. There she meets a number of fascinating characters, including a scarecrow without a brain, a tin woodman without a heart, and a lion without courage.

Baum teamed with artist W.W. Denslow for the book illustrations, and in 1900 "The Wonderful Wizard of Oz" was published. The first edition of ten thousand copies sold out before the book even arrived on bookstore shelves. A subsequent twenty-five thousand copies had equal success. Two years later, the book was adapted for the stage and debuted at Hamlin's Grand Opera House in Chicago. Much of the book's content was revised to suit adult audiences, with an emphasis on music over storyline.

In 1939, Hollywood studio Metro-Goldwyn-Mayer released "The Wizard of Oz" based on Baum's book. It starred child star Judy Garland as Dorothy, dancer Ray Bolger as the Scarecrow, actor Jack Haley as the Tin Woodman, and comedian Bert Lahr as the Cowardly Lion. Victor Fleming directed.

At two million dollars, a monumental cost for the time, the film was MGM's most expensive film ever. Disappointedly for the studio, "The Wizard of Oz" was not a box office hit, bringing in slightly over three million dollars during its original release.

It disappointed too in the 1939 Academy Awards. Although film critics had widely praised the production, especially for its makeup and costuming, "The Wizard of Oz" won only two Academy Awards. One of those was Best Original Song for "Over the Rainbow."

Like fine wine, reaction to the film has improved with age. Today it is lauded as one of Hollywood's best loved films. The American Film Institute's list of Top 100 films ranks it at number 10.

Over the ensuing decades, "The Wizard of Oz" has been staged by theatre companies around the world. In 2012, in collaboration with composer Andrew Lloyd Webber, Mirvish Productions of Toronto brought a new production of "The Wizard" of Oz to Canadian audiences.

A trio of Norfolk Terriers, owned by Terry and Jennifer Shevchenko of London, Ontario, shared the role of Toto, Dorothy Gale's beloved dog.

xxx

In 2006, when Terry Shevchenko retired from Sara Lee Company as a business development manager, he was looking for something to fill his time. One day, out for a walk with his Norfolk Terrier Tilley, he stopped to observe a group of dog fanciers engaged in the sport of dog agility. "I thought: 'that would be fun,'" recalled Terry, who immediately signed Tilley up for the fast-paced sport.

Despite her diminutive size, Tilley, smart as a whip and highly trainable, excelled at the sport. One day Terry was approached by a fellow member of The Middlesex Agility Club, Suzanne Hennessy.

> She told me that London's Grand Theatre was looking for a dog to play Toto in their upcoming production of "The Wizard of Oz". She suggested that Tilley might be great to play the role and we should audition. I was interested and followed through.

The little bundle of energy soared at the auditions and was the hands-down favourite to play the role. It was a big order for a mite of a dog to fill: 7 weeks of performances, for a total of 55 shows.

XXX

Over the coming weeks of rehearsals, Terry and Tilley worked hard learning the Toto part. It involved Tilley trotting on and off stage on command; staying; sitting on a stool; and walking alongside the characters. "It was important that the dog didn't bring the quality of the performance down," says Terry. Tilley also needed to relate to Dorothy onstage.

> My job was to get Tilley on and off stage at the appropriate times. But the actress who played Dorothy would be in control of her while she was on the stage. So there had to be good chemistry between them. They had to bond.

Actress Adrienne Merrell, in the Dorothy role, was up to the challenge. "But she carried dog treats in a special pocket in her dress to make sure this worked," laughs Terry. There were other variables too with which Tilley needed to gain comfort: noise, lights, props and movement of sets. Then there were the pyrotechnics! In the movie version, the Wicked Witch of the West arrives in a cloud of smoke and noise, as Dorothy is holding Toto in her arms.

This didn't work well for Tilley. "The pyrotechnics during the Wicked Witch's entry and exits panicked her," says Terry, "and we made the decision to keep her offstage during that time."

By opening night, Terry was sure of one thing: "Tilley was a real performer and loved being on stage." The audience loved her too and the biggest applause was always saved for the little dog.

XXX

After the Grand production closed, Tilley and Terry returned to a more mundane life. And neither of them liked it much. Terry started keeping his eyes open for other acting opportunities. Meanwhile Tilley and her new Norfolk Terrier brothers, Winny and Neddy, continued with dog agility until some acting roles became available.

Terry also worked at training the new dogs on basic commands, in the hopes that they might get their moment in the spotlight too. Still Tilley was the undisputed star. She got her chance to shine again playing Little Orphan Annie's dog Sandy in London's Original Kids production of Annie Warbucks. She then reprised the role of Toto in Drayton Productions' "The Wizard of Oz" in St. Jacobs and Grand Bend.

XXX

By early 2012, the word was out in theatrical circles that the lavish Andrew Lloyd Webber version of "The Wizard of Oz" currently wowing audiences in London, England, was coming to Canada. Mirvish Productions would be doing their best to repeat the London success with Canadian audiences.

The rumours became more substantial, with news that the search for the new Dorothy would be conducted through a reality television talent search on CBC called "Over the Rainbow." After an exhaustive multi-week production, singer/actress Danielle Wade was announced as the choice.

Concurrently, Mirvish began their search for Toto. But Terry Shevchenko was ahead of the game. He'd already been making calls, preparing his resumé and references. He also moved into high gear, training his trio of dogs.

> If we were chosen to play Toto, my hope was to have all three dogs share the role. Tilley would be lead actor, with Neddy sharing the role. Winny would be their understudy. With over two hundred and seventy shows during a ten-month run, it would be easier on the dogs to share the role.

Terry felt Tilley had a good chance of being chosen for the canine role of a lifetime. Experience and familiarity made Tilley, at least, a shoo-in for an audition. The breed of dog, the Norfolk Terrier, was looking good as an asset too. For the London, England, run, Toto had been played by a white West Highland Terrier. At a solid 28 pounds, the Westie was a heavy load for Dorothy to carry. The Mirvish folk were looking for a smaller dog to play in the Toronto production.

There were high celebrations in the Shevchenko family when they got word in July 2012 that the Norfolks had been chosen as the Mirvish Productions' Totos. Terry decided that Tilley, the old pro, would take the more demanding opening act, with Neddy and Winny, the newcomers, sharing the second act.

Logistics were the first order of business once the contract had been signed. For Tilley's previous gigs, the distance between London and Toronto was too far to commute. But because housing expenses weren't part of the contract with Mirvish, Terry didn't want to use up all the dogs' salary on rent. After a short stay at a friend's area home, Terry and the dogs moved into a relative's Toronto home. They would live there when the show was running—from Tuesday to Sunday—then return to London after Sunday's matinee. It would be a hectic, tiring schedule but the honour was worth the price to pay.

xxx

Rehearsals for the show began on November 20th, 2012. In addition to learning her lines, songs and dance steps, lead actress Danielle Wade had to bond with the Totos. The rest of the cast had been instructed not to interact with the dogs at all, ensuring the bond between Toto and Dorothy. Danielle carried special treats in a pocket of her dress too.

The dogs' rehearsals were coming along nicely, but as the show's first preview loomed, Terry became increasingly worried about the pyrotechnics—or the lack of them.

> The dogs hadn't been exposed to the Toronto pyrotechnics—the sound, smoke and lights. The first time they used them was during the first preview. Not surprisingly, the dogs reacted poorly. They were terrified, Neddy especially. It was a horrible experience for them. And I was so mad, so upset, at

> the lack of consideration for the dogs.

Seven shows passed before the show's director agreed to have Toto offstage with the arrival and departure of the Wicked Witch of the West—and the resulting pyrotechnics. But for at least one of Terry's dogs, the damage was done. "Winny never recovered and I needed to take him out of the show entirely," says Terry. It was a large disappointment.

Still in retrospect, the Mirvish Wizard of Oz experience was "thrilling," says Terry. His main "girl" Tilley was a trouper—and a star. In an interview with the Toronto Star Terry explains what made his dog such a natural on the stage:

> Tilley is the type of dog who wants to do things and she enjoys life to the limits. She lives large...and is a little diva; you can see the smile on her face. She just eats this stuff up. I am so proud of her.

Both handler and dogs relished the audience attention too.

> Before the shows I'd take the dogs out for walks along the Toronto streets or in parks. And of course people recognized them. After the show we always came outside of the theatre and say hi to the audience and let them meet the dogs. People loved it.

The Mirvish production of The Wizard of Oz closed its Toronto run in late August 2013. The cast and crew now prepared to go on tour throughout the U.S. But it would leave without Terry Shevchenko and his Totos. "We wanted to go on tour, but Troika Entertainment is using American dogs and handler," Terry says. It was not what Terry had hoped for.

But the taste of the limelight lingers and Terry is keeping his eyes open for other opportunities for his Norfolk Terriers. "We're looking at television and movie work too," he says. At age ten, Tilley is still raring to go. Terry continues to work with Neddy and Winny. "So keep your eyes open for us," he suggests.

LOVE!

Mourning for Cats

Margaret Atwood

Author of more than 50 volumes of poetry, children's literature, fiction and non-fiction, Margaret Atwood is undoubtedly one of Canada's most eminent and recognizable literary voices. She was born in Ottawa and raised in Northern Ontario, Quebec and Toronto, where she attended Victoria College at the University of Toronto. Margaret took her Master of Arts degree at Radcliffe College in Massachusetts.

She began her professional career in 1964 as a lecturer in the English Department of the University of British Columbia, and concluded this chapter of her life in 1972, as an associate professor of English at York University in Toronto.

Writing has been her life's work since this time. Best known for her novels, including "The Edible Woman", "The Handmaid's Tale", "The Robber Bride", "Alias Grace" and "The Blind Assassin", her work has been published in more than 40 languages and is required reading in university courses across Canada, the United States and Europe.

An innovator too, Atwood co-invented the Long Pen™ in 2004. This remote device facilitates audio and video conversation between writers and their fans during book signings. It also allows the author to autograph books for fans at a distance.

Margaret Atwood lives in Toronto with writer Graeme Gibson. They are both admirers and protectors of birds. Her poem "Mourning for Cats" explores society's sentiments toward pets of the feline variety—a feeling with which the poet takes some umbrage.

Mourning for Cats

We get too sentimental;
over dead animals.
We turn maudlin.
But only those with fur,
only those who look like us,
at least a little.
Those with big eyes,
eyes that face front.
Those with smallish noses
or modest beaks.
No one laments a spider.
Nor a crab.
Hookworms rate no wailing.
Fish neither.
Baby seals make the grade,
and dogs, and sometimes owls,
Cats almost always.
Do we think they are like dead children?
Do we think they are part of us,
the animal soul
stashed somewhere near the heart,
fuzzy and trusting,
and vital and on the prowl,
and brutal towards the other forms of life,
and happy most of the time
and also stupid?
(Why most always cats? Why do dead cats
call up such ludicrous tears?
Why such deep mourning?
Because we can no longer
see in the dark without them?
Because we're cold
without their fur? Because we've lost
our hidden second skin,
the one we'd change into

when we wanted to have fun,
when we wanted to kill things
without a second thought,
when we wanted to shed the dull thick weight
of being human?)

Little Red Little, "Chief of Security"

Brad Martin and Donna Hayes

It came as no surprise to anyone that Brad Martin would gravitate to a career that centred on books. Books had been his addiction since childhood. After graduating from McGill, then graduate school at the University of Toronto, Brad started out as a sales representative for McClelland & Stewart Publishing. This most-respected of Canadian publishers represented the works of such literary icons as Farley Mowat, Pierre Berton and Margaret Atwood.

Brad then moved to Penguin Publishing; from there he went on to Bantam Doubleday Dell; then he landed at Random House. In 2012 Random House officially took over McClelland & Stewart, a move that, according to Toronto Life Magazine assured "Brad Martin's coronation as the king of the Canadian publishing industry...the master of all."

Most recently, Penguin and Random House have merged and Brad is chief executive officer of the newly formed Penguin Random House.

Married to Donna Hayes, publisher and CEO of Harlequin Books, Brad shares the couch with Red, the couple's 14-year-old longhaired Dachshund.

xxx

"Red's still a pretty happy guy," Brad Martin says, of his television NBA basketball–watching buddy, Red. "And he likes his steak." All in all, says Brad, "Red is doing well for a 14-year-old canine senior who is diabetic, has Cushing's disease, and is blind and mostly deaf."

Brad fondly recalls the circumstances of Red joining their family: It was Christmas time. Donna and her sister had taken the children to see Stuart Little at a movie theatre in a mall in Cambridge, Ontario. On the way out of the mall, they saw this tiny pup in the window of a pet store. He looked exactly like the dog the sisters had had as children, and Donna fell immediately in love with him. He was so little—small enough to fit in a pocket.

So with Donna's sister's encouragement, she told the pet store staff that she was very interested in buying the pup. She'd leave a deposit if they could hold him for a couple of hours while she talked to her husband. The store salespeople said "No"—holding pets was against their policy. If the lady wanted the dog, she had to get him now. Donna felt she couldn't make such a big decision alone and so left the store dogless.

After picking up Brad in Cambridge, they talked about the pup all the way home to Toronto.

> By the time we reached home, I was as convinced as Donna that this was the dog for us, so we turned the car around and headed back to Cambridge. Donna called the store from the car to make sure the pup was still there. And he was.

As Donna was arranging for the pup's purchase, Brad questioned pet store staff about their unusual "no hold" policy. "It appears that it really didn't exist," chuckles Brad. "The staff had just fallen in love with him so much they didn't want him to leave."

xxx

"Red" was an appropriate moniker, given the little one's lustrous, rich, auburn colouring. Soon Red's "always gotta see what's going on" personality earned him the title "Chief of Security."

Because both Brad and Donna left home during the weekday, they decided to cage Red until he was older and housetrained. Donna borrowed a holding crate from her brother, who had crated his Labrador Retriever when he was a pup. The holding pen was as big as a hockey arena for the diminutive Dachshund pup.

On her first day at work after the Christmas holidays, Donna was eager to see how Red was doing. She returned home at lunchtime with her friend Mary in tow. Donna was shocked to find an empty cage. A search of the house ensued, and Red was found. Brad explains the mystery:

> Donna couldn't imagine how Red could have gotten out, so she decided to put him back in the crate and hide so he thought she was gone. She watched as he shimmied two feet up the side of the wire cage and escaped through a small opening in the top. A Lab could have barely put a paw through, but Red could get right out.

The cage was dispensed with and Red was never was placed in it again.

xxx

The Martins own a cottage near Lake Huron and there Red took on his position of Chief of Security. Of prime importance was keeping the cottage dock free of pesky ducks. Brad and Donna were entertained watching their dog spring into action, short little legs churning, ears flying as he made a rush towards the dockside interlopers.

> The first few times he'd get going so fast he had no way of stopping. So Red would continue right off the end of the dock and into the lake. I found out he could swim though, because he did the dog paddle till I could scoop him out of the water.

xxx

Into his 12th year, Red started drinking copious amounts of water; he appeared ravenous for food and needed to urinate frequently. His usual lustrous coat was dull and shedding. A trip to the veterinarian diagnosed Cushing's disease. Dachshunds are prone to this condition. Cushing's (in both dogs and humans) occurs when the adrenal gland begins to produce too much of the hormone cortisol.

Red's medical situation became more complicated when he developed diabetes at age 13. And so the Martin household needed to adjust to Red's special needs. In hot weather, even with household air conditioning, Red preferred to lie low in the basement family room where it was cooler. He submitted willingly to twice-daily insulin injections for the diabetes and daily oral medication for the Cushing's. "Red's a 'holds-no-grudges' kind of dog," say Brad, with fondness.

Blindness is a complication of diabetes in both humans and dogs. By 14, Red was going blind. "We knew when he started bumping into furniture and our legs," says Brad. Diabetes has caused cataracts in both Red's eyes. It has also destroyed one of Red's retinas, leaving him completely blind in one eye and with a loss of at least 80 percent vision in the other eye.

And if Red, Chief of Security, had not enough to deal with in his golden years, he began to lose his hearing as well. But the old trooper has developed coping strategies to deal with this challenge too. "He can't hear or see us when we come home after being away," reports Brad. "But he can feel the vibrations in the floor. So he'll still come to greet us. Red's an adaptable guy!"

Red's sensory losses have shaken his confidence though.

> He used to be quite independent and would go off on his own somewhere if Donna and I were both sitting down watching TV or reading. Now he likes to be close to us; he likes to know where we are in the house.

The Martins had considered surgery for Red's blind eye, but then decided against an operation.

> Given his age and his other medical conditions, we consulted

> with his wonderful veterinarian, Dr. Greg Usher, and decided that the stress on him would just be too much. The diabetes and Cushing's are stable, and the surgery would just upset this balance.

Instead, they'll give their treasured pal the best medicine of all: love, good medical care, the occasional steak dinner and summer trips to the cottage.

While the old guy can't see the pesky ducks on the dock or hear them, thanks to his fine "badger dog" nose, he can smell them a mile away!

Wiz

Dr. Stanley Coren

Dr. Stanley Coren is best known as an expert and lecturer on companion animal behaviour. However, as a professor of Psychology at University of British Columbia, his expertise goes much farther than dogs with separation anxiety and cats that overeat.

The author of more than three hundred scholarly papers in professional journals such as The British Journal of Medicine, the Psychological Review and The New England Journal of Medicine, his research includes studies on human vision and hearing, handedness, sleep and birth stress.

Stanley Coren's textbook, "Sensation and Perception", has long been the most used text in North American university and college courses on sensory and perceptual processes.

Dr. Coren has authored numerous books on companion animals. They include: "How to Speak Dog", "How Dogs Think", Do Dogs Dream?" and "The Intelligence of Dogs".

He's taken his knowledge and advice to television and has appeared on Oprah Winfrey, Larry King, Canada a.m., Good Morning America and The Today Show. He acted as host on the series Good Dog for the Life Network.

Dr. Coren is an instructor with the non-profit Vancouver Dog Obedience Training Club and a supporter of the SPCA, participating in their fund-raising and finding homes for shelter dogs.

He and his wife, Joan, live in Vancouver. They have three dogs and a cat.

The following story combines humour, words of caution and timely food for thought.

XXX

A Dog and a Murder Most Foul

According to the Zoroastrian religion that began in ancient Persia, the god Yima has set two four-eyed dogs to guard Chinvat Bridge, which is known as the "Bridge of Decision" between this world and heaven. These dogs are placed there because they, like all dogs, are good judges of character. It is said that will not let anyone pass on to Paradise if they have deliberately harmed a dog in this world.

If this is true there was a moment in time when my own entry to paradise was in jeopardy, especially if these dogs chose to gather their information from sources such as the Internet. I invite you to think of the following experience as a tale of wildlife and bloody murder.

Regardless of how large and built up a city may be, there will always be a number of wild animals that co-exist with the human population right in the heart of the metropolis. Some, like birds, are visible. Some, like rats and mice, we know are there, although we seldom see them. Other, more exotic animals, are also present, especially in large parks or undeveloped areas.

For example, I live in Vancouver whose metropolitan area contains well over two million people. I also live within a mile or so of a large city park. It's not all that unusual for me to see raccoons crossing the street in the early morning or when I drive home from work. One late night I even saw a coyote, walking down the middle of a street in our quiet residential area. Coyotes have become a bit of a problem in our city, since they sometimes view free-roaming cats or small dogs in backyards as potential menu items.

One Saturday afternoon I was working at home analyzing some data from my laboratory at the University of British Columbia. The problem I was working on was convoluted and complex and, although I felt I was making progress, the answer was still far from clear. I had been working on the computer since before 6 a.m. and it was now around 1 p.m. I was tired and had developed a headache. I took a couple of aspirin and, since the day was bright and pleasant, I decided to take my dog, Wizard, out for a walk to allow my head to clear.

At that time I only had one dog, my Cavalier King Charles Spaniel, Wiz. My bouncy Cairn Terrier, Flint, had recently died and my handsome Flat Coat Retriever, Odin, was still in his mother's womb and would not appear on the scene for a few weeks. Walking with Wiz was never an athletic event, since he moved no faster than a gentle stroll at any time.

Today I appreciated it since my mind was still involved with my analytical problem and this gave me time to think. I occasionally glanced at my pretty chestnut-and-white-coloured dog as he sniffed his way along, but otherwise I was not really paying much attention.

Because my mind was elsewhere and Wiz was at the far end of a long extendable leash, I never saw the actual encounter. I was jolted from my musing by Wiz's yelp of surprise and distress, which was followed seconds later by the unmistakable and unpleasant odour of skunk spray. Wiz dashed back from the bush that he had been sniffing, bringing an intense wave of that noxious odour with him.

I quickly looked him over to make sure he had no bites or injuries. Although Wiz was vaccinated I still worry about rabies, which can be carried by skunks. I also looked at Wiz's eyes, which were large and prominent as in all members of his breed, and fortunately they were clear. Skunk spray does bad things to a dog's eyes and can cause temporary blindness and long-term irritation. I could see that the faint yellow slick of skunk spray had hit his neck and one side of his body.

I gave a tug on Wiz's leash and started home at as fast a trot as I could coax from him. Fortunately, we were only a few city blocks from my home. I did deviate from the fastest route by crossing the street when a mother with a baby in a stroller approached—there is no benefit in exposing a child to the odour of skunks at that early age. Attracted by the sight of me trying to trot with a resistant and distressed dog, and also puzzled by the stench that hovered over us, several neighbourhood kids approached.

"Don't touch him," I warned them. "Skunk spray is an oil that spreads really easily and is difficult to get off. I just have to get him home and cleaned quickly. If you leave the spray on too long it gets into the hair and skin and then you can have it stinking up the place for months."

The kids backed off at my warning, but followed me out of curiosity.

xxx

Once home, rather than going inside, I rang the doorbell. My wife Joan appeared a couple of moments later and after one sniff she knew what the problem was. "Don't bring him into the house," she said with a sound of disgust in her voice. "There is tomato juice in the cupboard," she added.

I handed her the leash and dashed inside. I quickly changed into an old shirt and ripped jeans that I wouldn't mind losing if the smell couldn't be washed out. I then grabbed a large can of tomato juice and some liquid dishwashing detergent. I returned to the door and took the leash and Wiz.

We walked down the steps and around the house to the yard, followed by a small entourage of neighbourhood children. By the time I got to the rear Joan had reappeared with a yellow plastic wading pool, used by our grandchildren to play in. She was also trailing the garden hose behind her.

I put on some rubber gloves and slipped Wiz into the plastic walled container. We had always been told that the way that you deal with skunk smell on a dog is to soak them in tomato juice. In any event, that was the only remedy that either of us could think of at the moment. So I began to splash my unhappy dog with the contents of the can.

The kids who were watching thought this was hilarious, and giggled while I poured the heavy red liquid over him. It made Wiz look as if he were hemorrhaging blood from a series of massive wounds. Although my dog was obviously distraught, he eventually accepted the situation and, after a while lay down passively on his side. His only movements from then on were an occasional glance up at me with an expression that seemed to ask if this day could possibly get any worse.

While I waited for the tomato juice to soak in and do its work, one of the neighbourhood kids produced a camera and ran around snapping a few photos. I then started the work of washing Wiz down with the liquid detergent. The pink-coloured suds looked a lot more comforting than the pools of blood-like tomato juice.

The kids wandered off after I had dried Wiz with a towel. I anointed him with a couple drops of vanilla to mask any residual odour. Then I returned to my office where Wiz curled up at my feet and quietly fell asleep. Perhaps it was the surge of adrenalin or the physical activity, however, once back at the computer my previous problem seemed to solve itself, so I quietly thanked the skunk for his contribution.

What I could not know, was that the faint click of the camera shutter during Wiz's tomato juice bath would echo loudly over the next couple of weeks.

xxx

Around this time, one of the teachers in a nearby school had hit upon an interesting way to encourage her students to do more writing. Rather than having them write traditional essays, she had each create an individual website. This was so that each student could maintain a blog—a kind of web diary. Here students would write about their hobbies, likes and dislikes, family activities, current events or simply amusing or interesting items that they had encountered. Each student was required to make a minimum of three entries per week and the teacher would monitor, grade and critique their entries over the semester.

One of the students in this class happened to be the kid with the camera during Wiz's skunk decontamination bath. In an attempt at humour, he posted one of the photographs he had taken as part of an article with the headline "A Horrifying Case of Animal Abuse?" The text of the article went on to say that a well-known psychologist, supposedly an expert in dog behaviour and a friend of canines, was caught on camera engaging in bizarre activities that this psychologist claimed were designed to relieve his dog of a noxious problem.

Furthermore he did so in front of an astonished crowd of neighbours. It finished with the photograph of Wiz lying forlornly in his yellow plastic tub, his fur covered in red liquid streaks and a giant puddle of red fluid around him. It looked for all the world like he had been killed by some deranged beast that had left him lying in a pool of his own blood. The final sentences of the piece finished with "Can this be considered some kind of useful treatment or is this bloody murder? Ask the Doctor."

The student sent me an email linked to his web posting. I looked at it and thought that the picture did, in fact, look like a gruesome killing. I felt that the humour was a bit heavy-handed, and I wondered why, at no point in the piece, did he try to clue the reader into the fact that the red liquid was tomato juice being used to rid a dog of skunk odour. However, as an educator myself I noticed that the vocabulary and sentence structure were good and it appeared to me that the teacher's plan to improve the writing of her students was working. In the end I passed it off as just another of life's happenings.

A few days later I received a phone call at my office in the university from the teacher who was having the students write the blogs.

She wanted to know if I had seen the posting because she was clearly distressed about it.

"I was quite upset to see the evidence of animal abuse that my student collected," she stated. "Not many psychologists in this area other than you work with dogs, and I need to know if this event involved you or someone else that you may be acquainted with." "Didn't you ask the student to explain the circumstances around that photo and how he came to get it?" I replied.

"He told me that he felt that by posting material on his blog he was in effect a journalist and had the right to 'protect his sources.' I couldn't convince him otherwise, so I have reported the matter and forwarded his posting and the picture to the SPCA and the police."

I had a sinking feeling in my stomach. If I admitted that the posted photo was of my dog, at the very least the SPCA and the police would feel it necessary to follow up on the incident report by questioning me. If it got out into the media that I was being interrogated because of a charge of animal abuse this could be both embarrassing and damaging to my reputation.

This is because many people consider the simple fact that a name is mentioned in association with a criminal investigation as evidence that the person is guilty of that crime regardless of any later proof to the contrary. I did not want to lie to the teacher but I felt that the problem could be resolved without involving the authorities or potentially the press.

So I carefully replied, "I certainly did not engage in animal abuse, nor do I know of any other psychologists in this area who have done so."

She accepted my statement and my promise that I would try to clarify the matter. She was obviously still upset and angry when she hung up the telephone. I immediately emailed the student and told him what happened. Rather than be harsh and threatening I simply suggested that it might make an interesting second posting on his blog to let his readers in on the joke.

Fortunately, he agreed, and that same day, additional photos showing my hand pouring tomato juice from the can onto Wiz, then the later detergent scrub with the pink foam, appeared on his website. Along with that was an explanation that the incident was in response to a skunk attack. He must have cropped the photos, since my head or face were never visible. He also had the journalistic reserve to leave my name out of the article. I assume that the teacher accepted this entry since I never heard from her again and was not questioned by any official agencies about this matter.

xxx

Unfortunately, some other people to whom I told the story alerted me to the fact that the original photo had been picked up by some animal rights groups and presented on their websites as "evidence" of the fact that psychologists are abusing and killing animals as part of their research.

"After the new photos were posted I sat nursing a large glass of bourbon while I explained the day's events to my wife." Joan looked at me and said, "You didn't have to be so devious, you know. Why didn't you just invite the teacher over to show her that Wiz is alive and well?" I looked down at my dearly loved dog and shook my head. "I didn't want to have to explain the side effects of my tomato juice deodorant treatment," I said.

"What side effects?" was her puzzled response. "Look at him, Joannie, all of his lovely white fur is now bright pink and I don't have a clue how long the colour will last!"

Happily, a week and a half later, after three baths with a "whitening shampoo" for dogs, all of the pink evidence of my episode of "animal abuse" was erased from Wiz's fur. Unfortunately it was not erased from the Internet. I recently ran across that photo of Wizard's tomato juice bath still being used on an anti-animal cruelty website as evidence of vivisection and animal torture being done by psychologists.

I can only hope that if the dogs that guard the Chinvat Bridge come across that posting, they will give me a chance to explain what actually happened, rather than barring me from heaven because of it.

Acknowledgements

This book was a labour of love but could not have come to fruition without the assistance, support and input from many people. To you I send my gratitude.

To Ontario Veterinary College's Dean Elizabeth Stone I send my sincere thanks for allowing this project to be born and grow. Thank you for believing in me.

OVC's Pet Trust personnel were invaluable in preparing the book for publication--making sure all the "i's" were dotted and the "t's" were crossed. Thanks to Kim Robinson, Pet Trust's Managing Director, and Robin Van Alstine and also to Jane Dawkins, OVC Marketing and Communications Officer.

I'm indebted to a number of subjects in the book for their assistance in directing me to other pet-lovers. To Arlene Perly-Rae: You were the first Canadian Celebrity to say "yes" to my request to tell your pet story. You made me believe that this book could be a reality.

And to George and Susan Cohon—my first interviews for the book. Your enthusiasm to participate set the standards for others to come. A huge thank you for opening the door to a number of subjects.

Also to Brian Williams, Kurt Browning, Stanley Coren, Mary Walsh, Maureen Jennings and Mark Cohon for their referrals to other pet-loving Canadians .

A special thank you to Rick Hansen and his executive assistant, Connie Savage, who fought downtown Toronto traffic to meet me. And to Random House publisher Brad Martin for personally considering the book for publication.

And thanks to Shevaun Voisin for connecting me with Jann Arden—after many months of "digging."

And as always, I am grateful to my husband Louis Silcox, my personal chauffeur on innumerable trips down the 401 to Toronto interviews.

Nancy Silcox

New Hamburg, Ontario

About the Author

A former secondary school teacher and university counsellor, Nancy has been fully engaged in freelance writing for 15 years. Her first writing loves are history and biography. Since 2000 she's written six full-length biographies including ones on writer Edna Staebler and pioneering midwife Elsie Cressman. Her feature articles have been published in Grand and Most Magazines in the Waterloo Region; in the national magazines Arabella Design and Canada's History.

Nancy lives with her husband, Louis, outside New Hamburg, Ontario. Both dedicated to their beloved pets, they share their home with two Golden Retrievers and two rascally Siamese cats. Louis and Nancy recently purchased a cottage on Baptiste Lake in Haliburton so their pets could take in the northern air!

Photo and design credits:

Thank you to those interviewed for providing the wonderful collection of personal and family photographs found within this book.

Photo credits:
Margaret Atwood photo by Graeme Gibson
Chris Hadfield photo by Anya Chibis, www.anyachibis.com
Maureen Jennings photo by Iden Ford, Iden Ford Photography
Farley Mowat , Alice Painting by Donna Fan
Victoria Nolan photo by Joel Roger
Graeme Smith photo by Moe Dorion, The Globe & Mail
Totos photo by Terry Shevchenko
Brian and Geraldine Williams photo by Amy Williams
istockphotos - Pages 25, 43, 55, 61, 67, 73, 105
Dean Palmer, Dean Palmer Photography - Pages 81, 97, 111, 149, 155, 161, 169, 178, 195

All other photos provided courtesy of individuals interviewed.

Original paintings:

Tania Boterman is an OCAD graduate that worked as a Graphic Illustrator and Designer with Bruce Mau in Toronto, before exploring distant lands where she bartered paintings for haircuts and dinners.

While juggling painting and design commissions in Paris she fell in love with drawing animals, which began to feature prominently in her work.

Now returned to Toronto, Tania lives happily ever after — drawing furry little monsters, and laughing harder than everyone else. She continues her adventures with reckless abandon and would love to hear from you.

taniaboterman.com

Pet Trust aims to IMPROVE the health and well-being of all species by supporting promising discoveries at the Ontario Veterinary College.

About OVC Pet Trust:

OVC Pet Trust, founded in 1986 at the Ontario Veterinary College, University of Guelph is Canada's first charitable organization dedicated to the health and well-being of companion animals.

OVC Pet Trust honours the relationship between pets and their people and veterinary caregivers by raising funds to support innovative discoveries that improve the prevention, diagnosis and treatment of diseases of pets.

Funds also help train veterinarians to provide exceptional healthcare for pets and provide equipment and facilities for the Ontario Veterinary College.

OVC Pet Trust
Ontario Veterinary College
University of Guelph
50 Stone Road, Guelph ON N1G 2W1
General Inquiries: T. 519-824-4120 x 54695
ovcpet@uoguelph.ca
www.pettrust.ca

facebook.com/ovcpet @ovcpettrust

Charitable Registration Number: 10816 1829 RR 001

Recent works published by OVC

Animal Companions, Animal Doctors, Animal People

Edited by Hilde Weisert and Elizabeth Arnold Stone

ISBN: 9780889555983

An anthology of poems, stories, essays. Blending a mix of writers including poets Lorna Crozier, Mark Doty, Patrick Lane, and Molly Peacock with stories from everyday veterinarians and their clients. This book touches on such topics as the bond connecting veterinarians and animals, the never-ending "jobs" of the animals in our lives, and the role of animals in our imagination.

Sick! Curious Tales of Pests and Parasites We Share with Animals

Edited by Elizabeth Arnold Stone and Cate Dewey, Illustrated by Tony Linka

ISBN: 9780889556096

In this collection of short stories, find out about the world of veterinarians and how they solve medical mysteries from the front-line of disease. Learn about the critical role veterinarians play in keeping us all safe! From our animals to our environment to ourselves. Topics include: the discovery of West Nile Virus, the monkey spreading Ebola virus, to tales of tuberculosis, rabies and Mad Cow Disease.

Milestones: 150 Years of the Ontario Veterinary College

by Lisa M. Cox, Peter D. Conlon , Ian K. Barker (Editor)

ISBN: 9780889556010

A brief synopsis of research achievements, teaching advances, people and events throughout the history of the Ontario Veterinary College (OVC). Learn more about the oldest veterinary college in Canada and the United States and how the OVC helped shape the veterinary profession. The book is filled with many photos, some never before published, and an insightful short description on each milestone.

CPSIA information can be obtained
at www.ICGtesting.com
Printed in the USA
LVIC06n0223281114
415984LV00001B/1